Evil

American Society of Missiology Monograph Series

Chair of Series Editorial Committee, James R. Krabill

The ASM Monograph Series provides a forum for publishing quality dissertations and studies in the field of missiology. Collaborating with Pickwick Publications—a division of Wipf and Stock Publishers of Eugene, Oregon—the American Society of Missiology selects high quality dissertations and other monographic studies that offer research materials in mission studies for scholars, mission and church leaders, and the academic community at large. The ASM seeks scholarly work for publication in the series that throws light on issues confronting Christian world mission in its cultural, social, historical, biblical, and theological dimensions.

Missiology is an academic field that brings together scholars whose professional training ranges from doctoral-level preparation in areas such as Scripture, history and sociology of religions, anthropology, theology, international relations, interreligious interchange, mission history, inculturation, and church law. The American Society of Missiology, which sponsors this series, is an ecumenical body drawing members from Independent and Ecumenical Protestant, Catholic, Orthodox, and other traditions. Members of the ASM are united by their commitment to reflect on and do scholarly work relating to both mission history and the present-day mission of the church. The ASM Monograph Series aims to publish works of exceptional merit on specialized topics, with particular attention given to work by younger scholars, the dissemination and publication of which is difficult under the economic pressures of standard publishing models.

Persons seeking information about the ASM or the guidelines for having their dissertations considered for publication in the ASM Monograph Series should consult the Society's website—www.asmweb.org.

Members of the ASM Monograph Committee who approved this book are:

Susan Maros, Affiliate Assistant Professor of Christian Leadership
Fuller Theological Seminary

Sue Russell, Professor of Mission and Contextual Studies
Asbury Theological Seminary

RECENTLY PUBLISHED IN THE ASM MONOGRAPH SERIES

George Shakwelele, *Explaining the Practice of Elevating an Ancestor for Veneration*
Peter T. Lee, *Hybridizing Mission: Intercultural Social Dynamics among Christian Workers on Multicultural Teams in North Africa*

Evil

A North Korean Christian Refugee Perspective

RYAN KLEJMENT-LAVIN
Foreword by Jamie Sanchez

American Society of Missiology Monograph Series 72

☙PICKWICK *Publications* • Eugene, Oregon

EVIL
A North Korean Christian Refugee Perspective

American Society of Missiology Monograph Series 72

Copyright © 2024 Ryan Klejment-Lavin. All rights reserved. Except for brief quotations in critical publications or reviews, no part of this book may be reproduced in any manner without prior written permission from the publisher. Write: Permissions, Wipf and Stock Publishers, 199 W. 8th Ave., Suite 3, Eugene, OR 97401.

Pickwick Publications
An Imprint of Wipf and Stock Publishers
199 W. 8th Ave., Suite 3
Eugene, OR 97401

www.wipfandstock.com

PAPERBACK ISBN: 978-1-6667-6906-7
HARDCOVER ISBN: 978-1-6667-6907-4
EBOOK ISBN: 978-1-6667-6908-1

Cataloguing-in-Publication data:

Names: Klejment-Lavin, Ryan, author. | Sanchez, Jamie, foreword.
Title: Evil : A North Korean Christian refugee perspective / by Ryan Klejment-Lavin ; foreword by Jamie Sanchez.
Description: Eugene, OR : Pickwick Publications, 2024 | American Society of Missiology Monograph Series 72 | Includes bibliographical references and index.
Identifiers: ISBN 978-1-6667-6906-7 (paperback) | ISBN 978-1-6667-6907-4 (hardcover) | ISBN 978-1-6667-6908-1 (ebook)
Subjects: LCSH: Christianity—Korea. | Evangelicalism—Korea.
Classification: BR1329 .K60 2024 (paperback) | BR1329 .K60 (ebook)

VERSION NUMBER 08/16/24

Contents

Foreword by Jamie Sanchez | vii
Acknowledgments | ix

1. Introduction | 1
2. Literature Review | 9
3. Research Methods and Procedures | 58
4. Participants | 72
5. Findings | 84
6. Discussion | 138

Appendix A: Informed Consent Form | 169
Appendix B: Consent Form (Korean) | 171
Appendix C: Interview Questions | 173
Bibliography | 175
Subject Index | 181

Foreword

TODAY IS JUNE 20, World Refugees Day. The United Nations established this day in 2001 as a day to acknowledge, honor, and celebrate refugees from around the world. It's fitting that I am writing the foreword for Ryan Klejment-Lavin's book, *Evil*, on this day. Ryan has written a challenging account of evil from the perspectives of his research participants who are North Korean Christian refugees.

I first met Ryan when he started his PhD at Biola University. I had started my faculty position in Intercultural Studies graduate department at Biola University the year before. As the program director for the PhD in Intercultural Studies, I served as Ryan's academic advisor, a professor in some of his classes, and as his supervisor when he was a teaching assistant in one of my classes.

Over time, I saw Ryan develop into an astute scholar who thought deeply about issues and cared just as deeply about people. It was evident that he was determined for his doctoral research to matter.

My own research is in the area of refugee studies. I teach a course on refugees, am currently working with some colleagues on a research grant concerning women refugees, and have conducted research in Europe with refugees. In light of our similar research interests, and because of our great working relationship, I also served as Ryan's dissertation supervisor, working closely with him as he developed his dissertation which he has now turned into this book.

There is not a region of the world untouched by the plight of refugees. Yet, much of what I read about refugees is often situated in Europe and

Foreword

Africa. By centering his research in Asia, Ryan has expanded my understanding of the global refugee population and has added to the ongoing academic understanding of refugees.

Evil is a sophisticated work of research. Based on his dissertation research, Ryan presents a description of how North Korean Christian refugees describe their view of evil, particularly in light of their experiences as refugees. Yet, although *Evil* is an academic research book, it is also very accessible to the readers. One way Ryan ensures readers will connect with the book is by providing profiles of each of his research participants, allowing the reader to get to know, at least in part, about the men and women who entrusted their stories to Ryan, and by extension, to his readers.

Ryan's expertise of living in South Korea and as an expert on cultural studies is peppered throughout the pages of *Evil*. His sophisticated discussion of, *Juche*, a recently developed political ideology in North Korea is enlightening. His discussion of *Juche*, in light of his research findings demonstrates how well Ryan understands this area of the world.

I hope you will read *Evil* with your eyes and hearts wide open. Those interested in refugee studies will learn surely learn some keen academic insights into the plight of refugees fleeing North Korea. Those interested in refugees, as people, not just an academic field of study, will develop a deeper compassion and admiration for what some refugees have endured. Finally, readers will be reminded, even challenged by the research participants, to not let evil overcome them but to keep focused on our God who has indeed overcome evil.

Jamie N. Sanchez, PhD
Biola University
June 20, 2024

Acknowledgments

THIS BOOK IS THE culmination of years of study and has been influenced and impacted by a great number of people. Foremost, I would like to thank my dissertation chair, Dr. Jamie Sanchez, who has poured countless hours into guiding me and helping to craft my study into what it is today. I would also like to thank the other members of my committee, Dr. Leanne Dzubinski and Dr. Alan McMahan, for their input and encouragement.

There are a number of individuals and organizations that have assisted me with finding participants and understanding the context of North Korean Christian refugees, most of which cannot be named for security reasons. Suffice to say, you know who you are, and I am deeply grateful for your help and support. In particular, I want to thank the participants in this study who have trusted their stories with me. I hope and pray that this research will both contribute to the well-being of your communities, and encourage you in your faith, as you have encouraged me in my faith.

A special thanks is due to Dr. Harris Kim, Edwin Kang, and Tony Chung, who have offered plenty of encouragement, entertainment, and inspiration during this journey. Likewise, Sam and Lily, Rose and Wally, Sammi, and Dave have continued to spur me on and offer support when needed. I am indebted to Dr. Eunice Hong, who helped me better understand the coding and research process, and to Joy Choi, who has helped me many times with proofreading and feedback.

My PhD and dissertation would not have been possible without our team of supporters who continue to offer prayers and finances for our ministry. Thank you to each and every one of you. I am especially grateful

Acknowledgments

for the continued support and prayers from my parents, Dr. David and Debra Lavin.

Lastly, I want to thank my family, my wife Carolyn and our boys Noah and Finn, who sacrificed so much for me to complete this journey. Carolyn, you've been my number one cheerleader and have done so much to enable me to complete this PhD. I am forever grateful for you. Noah and Finn, I know you both have been waiting for daddy to be done with school so I have more time to play; daddy is done now.

1

Introduction

SEVERAL YEARS AGO, I was at a youth gathering in South Korea, bringing together North Korean and South Korean high school students to help build bridges. A keynote speaker began to introduce the realities of suffering in North Korea to the group. The atmosphere in the room shifted dramatically. The South Korean students were horrified at the stories of persecution and suffering that they were being told. All the while, the North Korean students seemed somewhat distant, not really wanting to engage with what were obvious past traumas.

The keynote speaker then gave an explanation why God would allow such suffering. It was obvious, he said. North Korean Christians bowed to Japanese Shinto shrines during the Japanese occupation of Korea, while South Korean Christians were faithful to God and did not bow to the shrines. According to the speaker, the suffering in North Korea is God's judgment on the country, being poured out for the last seventy years.

I was shocked. I watched this man stand in front of a group of youths and declare that what half of them had suffered was God's judgment on something that happened seventy years prior. This sounded more like the official North Korean *Juche* ideology, that demands three generations of political prisoners be punished for the crime of one, than the Gospel of the Lord Jesus.[1] My blood began to boil, and I directly told the youth in my group that I did not believe that. A question emerged though in our discussions: why did God allow the suffering to occur?

---

1. Emery et al., "After the Escape," 999–1022.

Evil: A North Korean Christian Refugee Perspective

Over the following years, I continued to meet and work with some North Korean refugee students. Several times I was asked the question, "Why is there evil?" This theological question arises when the reality of evil and suffering in the world is juxtaposed with the belief in an omnipotent, omniscient, and good God.[2] In one instance, I began to answer from my own understanding of the problem of evil; namely that God desires authentic love, and for there to be authentic love there must be free will, which necessitates an option to choose evil.[3] During my explanation, I was interrupted by the translator who told me that he disagreed with my answer. In his view, God predestined the evil for his own good purposes. The students were seeking an answer, but became confused by the disagreement between the translator and myself. This experience led me to want to understand more about how evil is understood amongst North Korean refugees.

THE PROBLEM OF EVIL

Discussion and debate on the problem of evil is nothing new to Christianity in general, or Christianity in the Korean peninsula specifically.[4] Early church writers such as Justin Martyr, Irenaeus, Tertullian, and St. Augustine of Hippo all wrote on the problem of evil during the first four hundred years of the church.[5] The Korean church, likewise, has a number of surviving reflections on the problem of evil from the late eighteenth century up through the 20th century.[6] The writings from the Korean church all situate the problem of evil in the contemporaneous context of the writer: either the Catholic persecution, the Japanese occupation, or the Korean war.[7] Each of these contexts was a period of time when the church was experiencing evil and suffering.

More recently, studies have been conducted looking at the phenomenon of evil; how individuals experience evil;[8] what individuals believe

---

2. Mackie, "Evil and Omnipotence," 200.
3. Boyd, *Satan and the Problem of Evil*, 16.
4. Rausch, "Suffering History," 69–97.
5. Burns, *Christian Understandings*, 53–69.
6. Rausch, "Suffering History," 70.
7. Rausch, "Suffering History," 70–71.
8. Alford, *What Evil Means*, 1.

about evil;[9] understanding how individuals construct their views on evil;[10] and how evil and suffering may influence individuals' beliefs about God.[11] Some studies have been focused on human responsibility in evil,[12] while others have focused on spiritual responsibility in evil.[13] The literature demonstrates an interest in understanding how people understand evil.

NORTH KOREAN REFUGEES

The official governing ideology of North Korea is called *Juche*, which is commonly translated as "self-reliance."[14] Juche was developed by Kim Il Sung as his own take on Marxism designed for a North Korean context; however, some scholars regard *Juche* as a religion that worships the North Korean regime.[15] North Korea is often considered *sui generis* when it comes to human rights violations.[16] Refugees from North Korea corroborate and confirm the international governmental research that has been conducted on the conditions inside North Korea.[17] It is currently estimated that 80,000–120,000 men, women, and children are kept in horrendous conditions in the state gulag prison system.[18] People convicted of crimes can have up to three generations of their family imprisoned with them to root out disloyalty.[19] Additionally, privation and starvation are widespread, with most North Koreans being affected.[20] It is these conditions that many North Koreans are fleeing.

---

9. Daugherty et al., "Measuring Theodicy," 43; Hale-Smith et al., "Measuring Beliefs," 855.

10. Bradshaw and Fitchett, "God, Why?," 179.

11. Bradley et al., "Relational Reasons for Nonbelief"; Bradley et al., "Reasons for Atheists and Agnostics"; Wilt et al., "God's Role in Suffering."

12. See Ahmadi et al., "Meaning-Making Coping"; Alford, *What Evil Means*.

13. See Bradley et al., "Relational Reasons"; Bradley et al., "Reasons for Atheists"; Bradshaw and Fitchett, "God, Why?," 179; Daugherty et al., "Measuring Theodicy," 43–44; Hale-Smith et al., "Measuring Beliefs," 855–56; Hall et al., "Theodicy or Not?"; Wilt et al., "God's Role in Suffering."

14. Belke, *Juche*, xiii.

15. Belke, *Juche*, 1–3.

16. UN Human Rights Council, "Special Rapporteur," 1.

17. UN Human Rights Council, "Special Rapporteur," 17.

18. US Department of State, "Country Reports," 6.

19. US Department of State, "Prisons," 1.

20. US Department of State, "Country Reports," 6.

Evil: A North Korean Christian Refugee Perspective

Yet, once a North Korean refugee arrives in South Korea, they are faced with additional challenges. In one empirical quantitative study, Kim et al. investigated the prevalence of post-traumatic stress disorder (PTSD), depression, and anxiety amongst refugees from North Korea who have arrived in South Korea.[21] The research findings suggest that the severity and prevalence of PTSD among the North Korean refugees are particularly high when compared with other refugees. This research confirmed that North Korean refugees who were caught and repatriated were subject to torture, detention, and brutal mental and physical punishment.[22]

A qualitative study, conducted by Yoo with North Korean refugees who were studying in seminary, identified the problem of evil as a particular issue on which the students needed training.[23] The North Korean seminary students "referred to the necessity of developing a biblical theology on particular themes such as theodicy and God's justice and blessings as understood in the Scriptures."[24] Additionally, the North Korean seminary students expressed hearing similar statements to the one I heard the keynote speaker make:

> A few consultants mentioned that when they were in China they heard that the poverty and famine in North Korea was divinely ordained. They alluded to similar discourses which claimed that North Korea's famine was due to the fact that it had abandoned God, while prosperity in China—just across the border from North Korea—and wealth in South Korea were due to their acknowledgement of God's existence.[25]

Furthermore, while there has been research on how Korean Christians have constructed their theological views on the problem of evil in the past,[26] there has been little, if any, research on how North Korean Christians understand evil.

---

21. Kim et al., "Pre-migration Trauma," 466.
22. Kim et al., "Pre-migration Trauma," 471.
23. Yoo, *Learning Experiences*, 279.
24. Yoo, *Learning Experiences*, 279.
25. Yoo, *Learning Experiences*, 280.
26. Rausch, "Suffering History," 70.

Introduction

PROBLEM STATEMENT

North Korean refugees have experienced intense physical and emotional traumas.[27] Many of these refugees are practicing Christians.[28] Prior research has highlighted the need in North Korean evangelism for a biblical theology of evil and suffering.[29] Prior research has also demonstrated belief in God is related to ideas about evil and suffering.[30] Additionally, existing scholarship has examined how particular groups understand evil,[31] and how different Christians have constructed a biblical theology of evil.[32] Though general ideas of a Korean theological understanding of evil can be found in literature, it appears that almost no scholarly research has been carried out to understand how North Korean Christian refugees describe evil based on their lived experiences.

PURPOSE STATEMENT

The purpose of the basic qualitative study was to understand how North Korean Christian refugees describe evil based on their lived experiences.

RESEARCH QUESTION

The central research question in this study was, How do North Korean Christian refugees understand and describe evil based on their lived experiences?

Sub-Questions

1. How do the participants understand and describe the causes of evil?

---

27. Kim et al., "Understanding Social Exclusion and Psychosocial Adjustment"; Kim et al., "Pre-migration Trauma"; Transitional Justice Working Group, *Exploring Grassroots*, 23.

28. Cho, "Effect of Religion"; Jun et al., "Understanding the Acceptance," 445; Chung, "Between Defector and Migrant," 21.

29. Yoo, *Learning Experiences*, 279–80.

30. Bradley et al., "Relational Reasons"; Bradley et al., "Reasons for Atheists"; Wilt et al., "God's Role."

31. Alford, *What Evil Means*, 1–6; Bradshaw and Fitchett, "God, Why?," 179; Daugherty et al., "Measuring Theodicy"; Hale-Smith et al., "Measuring Beliefs," 856–57; Hall et al., "Theodicy or Not?"

32. Alcorn, *If God Is Good*; Boyd, *Satan and the Problem of Evil*; Plantinga, *God, Freedom, and Evil*; Rausch, "Suffering History"; Wright, *Evil and the Justice of God*.

2. How do participants understand and describe the fallenness of humankind in light of evil?

3. How do the participants understand and describe the sovereignty of God in light of evil?

4. How do the participants understand and describe the goodness of God in light of evil?

DEFINITIONS

For the purpose of this study, the following definitions of certain key terms are used.

1. Ak (악): The Korean word for general evil, as used in the Lord's Prayer.

2. Divine Aikido: The belief that God does not cause harm, but allows the violence of humans to come back upon themselves.[33]

3. Hanawon (하나원): The government-sponsored three-month adjustment program for North Koreans who arrive in South Korea.[34]

4. *Juche*: The official ideology of North Korea which stresses self-reliance and loyalty to the nation and its leader.[35]

5. North Korean Refugee: Someone who was born in North Korea but has left and lives in South Korea. I recognize that this particular term is highly contested and politicized. My decision for using this term instead of defector, migrant, or resettler, is based on the status conferred upon North Koreans when they flee North Korea by the protocols of the United Nations High Commissioner for Refugees.[36]

6. Problem of evil: The theological question of how one reconciles evil and suffering with belief in an omnipotent, omniscient, and good God.[37]

7. Theodicy: An attempt to reconcile the character of God or the existence of God with the experience of suffering in the world.[38]

---

33. Boyd, *Crucifixion of the Warrior God*, 768–69.
34. Poorman, "North Korean Defectors," 103.
35. Belke, *Juche*, 7–10.
36. Chun, "Representation and Self-Presentation," 97.
37. Rausch, "Suffering History," 70.
38. Hall et al., "Theodicy or Not?," 263.

Introduction

8. Teleological: Referring to ultimate goals and the afterlife consequences of actions.[39]

SCOPE

The purpose of this study was to understand how North Korean Christian refugees understand evil based on their lived experiences. The scope of this study was delimited to individuals who were born in North Korea and currently live in South Korea, and who self-identify as Christian. Furthermore, the study was delimited to individuals who were more than twenty years old and have been in South Korea for at least one year. The purpose for these criteria is to allow for the arrival and adjustment process that all North Korean refugees must undergo. The participants have all been in South Korea between one and seven years. In all, interviews were conducted with 12 participants who fit these criteria.

LIMITATIONS

Conducting this qualitative study contained some challenges. First, not all the participants were fluent or comfortable to do interviews in English, and chose to speak in Korean. As such, an interpreter assisted with the interviews that were conducted in Korean. Doing interviews through interpretation may have impacted some mutual understanding. To address this, I often asked the same question in a different way to make sure that the interpreter, participant, and myself were understanding each other.

A second challenge is that participants may have felt reticent sharing their stories and views on evil with me, which would limit the data I was able to collect. To overcome this limitation, I sought to build relational rapport with prior participants to assist with establishing trust with future participants during data collection. I also made clear to the participants before each interview that nothing they would say would offend or shock me, and they could speak as freely as they wanted. As such, the data obtained from the interviews was both rich and substantial.

A third limitation would be my own personal bias regarding the understanding of evil, particularly when asked my own opinions by participants. To bracket this bias, I did not share my own views on evil with participants until after the interviews were conducted, and used thick and rich description in order to establish trustworthiness in this research. I will provide more details about this in Chapter 3.

39. Hall and Hill, "Meaning-Making," 469.

A fourth challenge was the COVID-19 epidemic. This data for this qualitative study was collected through semi-structured in-depth interviews. However, due to the outbreak of COVID-19 and social distancing requirements, in-person interviews were almost never an option. To overcome this challenge, I utilized Zoom to conduct all but one of the interviews remotely. In line with previous literature that demonstrated that conducting the interviews remotely does not negatively impact the data collection,[40] I was able to gather rich data through remote interviews.

A fifth limitation was that there were more female than male participants in this study. In all, nine females and three males were interviewed for this study. However, this is reflective of the population of North Korean refugees in South Korea, as according to the South Korean government, 72 percent of all North Korean refugees in South Korea are females.[41]

SIGNIFICANCE STATEMENT

I have not found any scholarly research that has been conducted regarding North Koreans and their views on evil. As such, this empirical research about the North Korean Christian refugee understanding of evil provides both contributions to theory and implications for practice.

Theoretical Significance

This research contributed to theory by advancing the study into specific groups' beliefs about evil and theodicy. Specifically, this study substantiated the assertions of Yoo that theodicy and evil were important topics for North Korean Christian refugees.[42] It also further added to and clarified existing scholarship on the North Korean refugee experience.

Practical Significance

This study also provided two substantial implications for practice, specifically regarding work among North Korean Christian refugees. The findings in this study may assist Christian ministries in the discussion of theodicy and theological answers to evil. Additionally, this study may help sensitize practitioners to the experience of North Korean Christian refugees.

---

40. Dzubinski, *Distance Interviews*, 64–65.
41. Ministry of Unification, "Policy on North Korean," 1.
42. Yoo, *Learning Experiences*, 279.

2

Literature Review

THE PURPOSE OF THIS basic qualitative study was to understand how North Korean Christian refugees describe evil based on their lived experiences. This literature review will frame the research by establishing the ways in which evil has been perceived in the Korean peninsula. These concepts may have influenced the perceptions and beliefs about evil that North Korean refugees have constructed. Additionally, the literature review will help to sensitize us to the issues surrounding evil in East Asia.

In order to get a broad view of the concepts that are associated with this research topic, I will look at five main genres of academic research: North Korean context, North Korean refugee experience, Korean religious history, Korean religious understanding of evil, and prior studies on evil. This research resides in the intersection where these five genres of literature meet and form a gap.

NORTH KOREAN CONTEXT

Formally named the Democratic People's Republic of Korea (DPRK), North Korea is a country governed by a hereditary dictatorship.[1] North Korea has a centrally directed and closed economy, with a population of twenty-five million who experience regular shortages in food and goods.[2] The Korean peninsula is divided by the DMZ, a four-kilometer-wide demilitarized zone

---

1. Central Intelligence Agency, "Korea, North," 1.
2. Central Intelligence Agency, "Korea, North," 1.

that is virtually impassable and separates North Korea from South Korea.[3] China and Russia both border the country to the North and offer the only land links to the outside world.

The reality of traumatic suffering as part of the North Korean experience has been established in an empirical quantitative study by Kim et al. With a large sample size of 698 participants, the study found that while 10–30 percent of refugees worldwide suffer from PTSD,

> the severity and prevalence of PTSD among the North Korean refugees are particularly high comparing with other refugees who were meta-analyzed by various prior studies. This high level of PTSD among the North Korean subjects is linked to their experienced pre-migration trauma.[4]

The study also showed that women have a higher propensity to experience PTSD than men, which may be due to specific gender-based experiences that occur on their journey to South Korea.[5]

Another empirical study was conducted by the Transitional Justice Working Group, which interviewed 450 North Korean escapees living in South Korea.[6] Using a mixed methods approach, the Transitional Justice Working Group used a questionnaire with the participants, followed up with in-depth interviews.[7] Out of the participants, 47.7 percent stated that they themselves experienced physical violence in North Korea, in the forms of beatings, torture, rape, and other sexual assault.[8]

Additionally, 75.4 percent of participants reported experiencing wider harm, which

> included experience of physical violence from the previous question and added on experience of the loss of a close family member to execution or starvation, forced repatriation to North Korea from another country, and arrest or detention by the North Korean authorities.[9]

---

3. Central Intelligence Agency, "Korea, North," 1.
4. Kim et al., "Pre-migration Trauma," 471.
5. Kim et al., "Pre-migration Trauma," 471.
6. Transitional Justice Working Group, *Exploring Grassroots*, 12.
7. Transitional Justice Working Group, *Exploring Grassroots*, 14–15.
8. Transitional Justice Working Group, *Exploring Grassroots*, 23.
9. Transitional Justice Working Group, *Exploring Grassroots*, 23.

Of the participants who reported experiencing harm, 63.4 percent stated that they still suffer the physical and psychological consequences of their experience.[10]

Emery et al. also conducted a mixed method study with North Korean refugees in South Korea.[11] The central research question of their study concerned the relationship between victimization by political violence against women in North Korea and later physical abuse of offspring.[12] Specifically, this study examined how suffering violence from the government authorities and PTSD are related to physical abuse of children. Using qualitative interviews and quantitative surveys with 204 North Korean refugee women in South Korea, the findings indicated that 63.2 percent of participants suffered from PTSD, while 21 percent of participants reported physical violence at the hands of North Korean authorities.[13]

Ulferts and Howard discussed the human rights situation in North Korea, and how, contrary to the motivations behind international policies towards North Korea, human rights abuses have only continued in spite of international outcry.[14] North Korean citizens lack freedom of speech, freedom of religion, freedom of movement, and political freedom. Dissidents are imprisoned or condemned to slave labor.[15]

Ulferts and Howard estimated that there are 150,000–200,000 political prisoners held in six giant prison camps,[16] slightly higher than the estimates of the U.S. Department of State.[17] Additionally, starvation has been a significant problem in North Korea, as international organizations estimate:

> Somewhere between 1 and 3 million North Koreans lost their lives as a result of food scarcity and related diseases in the 1990s. These estimates make it the greatest famine in modern history. In contrast, the Ethiopian famine of 1984–1985 claimed the lives of about 1 million people.[18]

---

10. Transitional Justice Working Group, *Exploring Grassroots*, 23.
11. Emery et al., "After the Escape," 999–1022.
12. Emery et al., "After the Escape," 1003.
13. Emery et al., "After the Escape," 1006.
14. Ulferts and Howard, "North Korean Human Rights," 89.
15. Ulferts and Howard, "North Korean Human Rights," 85.
16. Ulferts and Howard, "North Korean Human Rights," 86.
17. US Department of State, "Country Reports," 6.
18. Ulferts and Howard, "North Korean Human Rights," 86.

Evil: A North Korean Christian Refugee Perspective

While the food scarcity from the 1990s seems in the past, the study conducted by the Transitional Justice Working Group also identified starvation as widespread in North Korea.[19]

Another contributor to the discussion of the suffering of North Koreans was Wolman, who agreed with Ulferts and Howard on the number of political prisoners and considered it a prime example of the evil found in North Korea:

> Perhaps the signature evil of the North Korean regime is its system of six kwan-li-so prison camps, where an estimated 150,000 to 200,000 individuals are confined in extraordinarily brutal conditions without legal recourse. According to reports, at times multiple family members are imprisoned because of the actions of one person.[20]

Additionally, Wolman noted that Christians receive special persecution, with 50,000–70,000 imprisoned in camps.[21]

Regarding basic freedoms of North Koreans, Wolman again concurred with Ulferts and Howard that political freedom, religious freedom, freedom of assembly, freedom of speech, and freedom of movement are all highly restricted or non-existent.[22] While these statements may sound hyperbolic, they are corroborated in the Report of the Special Rapporteur about human rights in the Democratic People's Republic of Korea.[23]

Wolman concluded that the evidence of evil and suffering in North Korea is incontrovertible:

> There is no real debate about the fundamental gravity of North Korean human rights abuses, there is nevertheless considerable uncertainty about some of the details of those abuses, due to the closed nature of North Korean society.[24]

While there is uncertainty about some of the details of human rights abuses in North Korea, it is an accepted fact that those abuses are

---

19. Transitional Justice Working Group, *Exploring Grassroots*, 23.
20. Wolman, "South Korea's Response," 2.
21. Wolman, "South Korea's Response," 2.
22. Wolman, "South Korea's Response," 2.
23. UN Human Rights Council, "Special Rapporteur," 9–11.
24. Wolman, "South Korea's Response," 3.

Literature Review

widespread and extreme. Additionally, more recent research[25] has begun to empirically document the details that Wolman considered as uncertain.[26]

It is from this context of suffering in a closed-off country that thousands of North Koreans attempt to escape. I will now briefly review literature surrounding the North Korean refugee experience.

NORTH KOREAN REFUGEE EXPERIENCE

North Korea borders three countries: China, Russia, and South Korea. Due to the militarized border and the demilitarized DMZ corridor, defection directly into South Korea is rare. An article in *The Washington Post* documented the last known defection across the DMZ which occurred in 2017, when a North Korean soldier dramatically ran across the DMZ to South Korea under gunfire from fellow North Korean soldiers, sustaining five gunshot wounds.[27]

The coastlines of North Korea are also difficult to defect through. The shores are lined with barbed wire fences and patrolled by the North Korean Navy. As such, the coastlines are not a common route to use for defection, leaving the main route of fleeing North Korea through the northern border, most commonly into China.[28]

Escape Journey

To attempt to escape from North Korea is to take a great risk, both for the individual and for the individual's relatives.[29] Individuals caught attempting to escape face imprisonment or execution,[30] while family members who remain in North Korea can be subjected to imprisonment.[31] If anyone does successfully make it across the heavily guarded border into China, they must then avoid being caught or found by Chinese authorities.[32]

---

25. Kim et al., "Pre-migration Trauma"; Transitional Justice Working Group, *Exploring Grassroots*, 23–25; Transitional Justice Working Group, *Mapping the Fate*, 29–41.

26. Wolman, "South Korea's Response," 3.

27. Eltagouri, "What We've Learned."

28. Emery et al., "After the Escape," 1000.

29. Emery et al., "After the Escape," 1002.

30. Poorman, "North Korean Defectors," 100.

31. Emery et al., "After the Escape," 1002.

32. Lee, "Educational Experiences," 34.

Harboring a North Korean in China is illegal, as China formally considers any North Koreans fleeing from North Korea as economic migrants and not refugees.[33] This position is in contradiction to the position of the United Nations High Commissioner for Refugees, which considers any North Korean fleeing to be a legal refugee.[34] Therefore, North Koreans who attempt to defect need to contact individuals or groups who will assume the legal risk if they help.[35]

Often the groups willing to assume the legal risk are Christian churches.[36] After arriving in China, some refugees obtain forged documents to assume the identity of a Chinese citizen and can remain in China for several years. Other refugees make their way across China to another country where they can claim asylum and not be forcibly returned to North Korea.[37]

For the most part, North Koreans choose to seek asylum in South Korea.[38] Presumably this is due to the language and cultural similarity that North Koreans perceive they will find in South Korea, but also due to the benefits of claiming asylum in South Korea.[39] According to the South Korean constitution, North Koreans who arrive are not officially treated as refugees, but given citizenship and financial support.[40] The arrival and adjustment process for North Koreans to South Korea, however, is not an easy process and involves some hardships.

Arrival and Adjustment Process

As of 2020, there are over 33,500 North Korean defectors that have resettled in South Korea.[41] As previously stated, the majority of these have defected North Korea across the border into China, where they made their way to a third country to claim asylum.[42] Upon arrival in South Korea, North Korean refugees are put through an interrogation and investigation process to

33. Chun, "Representation and Self-Presentation," 97.
34. Chun, "Representation and Self-Presentation," 97.
35. Lee, "Educational Experiences," 34.
36. Jun et al., "Understanding the Acceptance," 445; Lee, "Educational Experiences," 39.
37. Poorman, "North Korean Defectors," 110.
38. Poorman, "North Korean Defectors," 110.
39. Poorman, "North Korean Defectors," 108.
40. Poorman, "North Korean Defectors," 102.
41. Ministry of Unification, "Policy on North Korean."
42. Yeom and Ward, "Integrating North Korean Refugee," 29–30.

Literature Review

ensure that the individual is, in fact, a North Korean citizen who defected, and also to catch any potential North Korean spies.[43] The interrogation and investigation process can take anywhere from one week to one month; if the individual is deemed to be non-threatening then that person is then moved to a government resettlement center called *Hanawon*.[44]

In *Hanawon*, the North Koreans learn how to live and adjust in South Korea. At *Hanawon*, the North Koreans

> go through a three-month educational program on life in South Korea. The lessons include how to take public transportation, how to open a bank account, and lessons on democracy and capitalism. Some defectors even elect to do a homestay with a South Korean family to acclimate to the country.[45]

After completing the program at *Hanawon*, North Korean refugees are officially given citizenship status in South Korea, along with the financial benefits, including housing and education subsidies.[46]

In addition to the official government program at the *Hanawon* center, several NGOs and non-profit organizations are working in South Korea to assist North Korean refugees with life and adjustment in Korea.[47] This is in part because of the obstacles that North Koreans face in South Korea.

As mentioned above, a few North Korean refugees have converted to Christianity after escaping North Korea.[48] Jun et al. conducted a mixed methods study to explore the factors or experiences that influence faith acceptance and growth amongst North Korean refugees in South Korea.[49] Using concept-mapping methods and in-depth interviews with North Korean refugee pastors in South Korea, Jun et al. found five key perceptions of the pastors as to why North Korean refugees come to accept the Christian faith.[50] These five findings were a personal encounter with God, individual identity, the active role of the church and pastors, the mutual relationship between South and North Korean Christians, and the alliance

---

43. Poorman, "North Korean Defectors," 103.
44. Poorman, "North Korean Defectors," 103.
45. Poorman, "North Korean Defectors," 103.
46. Ministry of Unification, "Settlement Support."
47. Poorman, "North Korean Defectors," 105.
48. Cho, "Effect of Religion," 21; Jun et al., "Understanding the Acceptance," 445.
49. Jun et al., "Understanding the Acceptance," 447.
50. Jun et al., "Understanding the Acceptance," 449.

between South and North Korean Christians.[51] The study suggested that the South Korean church has an important role in helping North Korean refugees who are Christians in South Korea form a healthy and adjusted faith community.[52]

Risks and Needs of Refugees

North Korean refugees in South Korea are disenfranchised in several ways. As a group, North Korean refugees are considered at-risk for sex trafficking and other types of exploitation.[53] This is compounded by the fact that many North Koreans cannot find adequate employment due to the lack of education, social capital, and a stigma that exists in South Korea against North Koreans.[54]

North Koreans experience disenfranchisement in education-crazed South Korea as well. North Koreans are offered special scholarships to top universities in South Korea, as well as easier entrance exams.[55] However, the North Korean education system is far behind the South Korean education system, which leaves North Korean refugees struggling in the South Korean education system and leads to a high dropout rate.[56]

Yeom and Ward conducted an empirical qualitative study with North Korean refugee students in South Korea.[57] After performing a needs assessment at the school where the North Korean refugees were students, Yeom and Ward "found there is a great array of needs among North Korean refugee youths in the South Korean educations system—curricular, social/cultural, psychological, medical, familial, communal, and political."[58] They further noted that North Korean refugee youths feel segregated from South Korean society at large and are only partly assimilated into South Korean culture.[59]

---

51. Jun et al., "Understanding the Acceptance," 449.
52. Jun et al., "Understanding the Acceptance," 450.
53. Yeom and Ward, "Integrating North Korean Refugee," 30.
54. Hamad, "Language Split," 24–25.
55. Ministry of Unification, "Settlement Support."
56. Yeom and Ward, "Integrating North Korean Refugee," 31.
57. Yeom and Ward, "Integrating North Korean Refugee," 31–32.
58. Yeom and Ward, "Integrating North Korean Refugee," 37.
59. Yeom and Ward, "Integrating North Korean Refugee," 38.

Literature Review

A mixed methods study conducted by Han et al. found a high prevalence of depression symptoms among North Korean refugees.[60] Some contributing factors include maladjustment to South Korean society, past trauma, and loneliness. Furthermore, high levels of unemployment among the North Korean refugee population are thought to increase their prevalence of depression and mental health issues.[61]

Kim and Atteraya conducted a quantitative study investigating factors associated with North Korean refugees' intentions to resettle permanently in South Korea.[62] The study found that North Korean refugees experience considerable levels of stress adjusting to South Korean society.[63] Additionally, the study found that the longer North Korean refugees live in South Korea, the less likely they are to settle there permanently.[64] Kim and Atteraya suggested that the longer North Korean refugees live in South Korea, the more discrimination and prejudice they experience, thus leading to lower levels of permanent settling.[65]

Women Refugees and Sexual Violence

An additional risk for refugees is the danger of sexual violence. Studies have shown that women refugees are at an increased risk for sexual exploitation and violence.[66] Williams et al. conducted a qualitative study with refugees in Rwanda.[67] The central research question of the study was to identify social and economic vulnerabilities of female adolescents in the refugee camps.[68] The study found that the convergence of poverty, lack of economic opportunity, and overall vulnerability led to sexual exploitation of women.

A more recent qualitative study was conducted by Gebreyesus et al.[69] In their study, Gebreyesus et al. conducted in depth interviews and focus group discussions with Eritrean refugees in Israel to explore the risk for

---

60. Han et al., "Depression in North Korean Refugees," 283.
61. Han et al., "Depression in North Korean Refugees," 287.
62. Kim and Atteraya, "North Korean Refugees' Intention," 1191–93.
63. Kim and Atteraya, "North Korean Refugees' Intention," 1194.
64. Kim and Atteraya, "North Korean Refugees' Intention," 1193.
65. Kim and Atteraya, "North Korean Refugees' Intention," 1197.
66. Gebreyesus et al., "Violence en Route," 721; Willams et al., "Child Protection and Sexual Exploitation," 162.
67. Willams et al., "Child Protection and Sexual Exploitation," 160.
68. Willams et al., "Child Protection and Sexual Exploitation," 160.
69. Gebreyesus et al., "Violence en Route," 721–43.

sexual violence experienced by women asylum seekers.[70] They found that the combination of movement through dangerous and isolated terrain, the dependence on human smugglers, and the vulnerability to traffickers led to a normalization of sexual violence.[71]

Kandemiri and Nkomo also conducted a qualitative study that highlighted the risk of sexual violence Congolese refugees faced.[72] The purpose of the study was to explore the role of forgiveness on the mental well-being of Congolese.[73] The study found that forgiveness improved mental well-being, but individuals who experienced or witnessed sexual violence or torture found it more difficult to forgive than individuals who had not experienced sexual violence or torture.[74]

KOREAN RELIGIOUS HISTORY

In order to understand Korean views regarding evil, I will first establish what philosophies and religions have been present or influential in the Korean peninsula. After the pertinent worldviews have been established, I will review the literature specifically surrounding those worldviews.

Eckert et al. have written an excellent book on Korean history, compiled by the foremost scholars from universities in the United States and South Korea.[75] Eckert et al. traced the major events and developments in the Korean peninsula from pre-history up through the 20th century. While the focus of the book is more on secular history than religious history, the development of the religious and philosophical traditions in Korea is covered therein.

Eckert et al. highlighted four main religious traditions in Korea: shamanism, Buddhism, Confucianism, and Christianity.[76] While the authors mentioned other minor cults or religions, none are considered as significant as the major four. Starting from pre-history shamanism, Eckert et al. traced the establishment of Buddhism as the preeminent religion in the peninsula,[77] with Confucianism providing the political and societal

70. Gebreyesus et al., "Violence en Route," 725–26.
71. Gebreyesus et al., "Violence en Route," 738.
72. Kandemiri and Nkomo, "Congolese Refugees and Asylum Seekers," 556–67.
73. Kandemiri and Nkomo, "Congolese Refugees and Asylum Seekers," 552.
74. Kandemiri and Nkomo, "Congolese Refugees and Asylum Seekers," 562–63.
75. Eckert et al., *Korea Old and New*, iii–iv.
76. Eckert et al., *Korea Old and New*, 409.
77. Eckert et al., *Korea Old and New*, 50.

Literature Review

structure for governments.[78] The authors demonstrated that in the late fifteenth century, Confucianism was established as the state religion,[79] while Buddhism underwent several repressions.[80] In fact, Christianity did not take significant root in the peninsula until the twentieth century, when it expanded rapidly.[81]

In a work examining only the religious history and movement in Korea, Buswell also arranged the religious traditions as Buddhism, Christianity, Confucianism, and Shamanism.[82] However, Buswell went further and included a whole category for new religions. Importantly, *Juche* is included in this category of new religions in the Korean peninsula, something that was entirely omitted from Eckert et al., due to the fact that their research did not cover the history of North Korea after the Korean war.[83]

More recently, Min organized the religions in Korea as simply the interplay between Buddhism, Confucianism, and Christianity, and noticeably omitted shamanism or any new religious movement.[84] The purpose of Min's work was to elucidate the interaction between these three faiths as they have coexisted in Korea, and not to be an exhaustive survey of the religions in Korea. Min posited that the interplay between the three faiths has been a combination of exclusion, practical accommodation, and assimilation, highlighting the influence the faiths have had on each other.[85] The positive interaction of the faiths as described by Min is in agreement with the assertion of Koehler, who also postulated that religious faiths in Korea have tended towards syncretism with each other.[86]

Grayson used a more inclusive approach to religious traditions in Korea and included many of the smaller cults and philosophical systems that have existed over the years.[87] While several of these smaller cults are not significant in the greater scheme of Korean religious history, Grayson did, however, contribute several important ideas to the discussion.

78. Eckert et al., *Korea Old and New*, 52.
79. Eckert et al., *Korea Old and New*, 129–30.
80. Eckert et al., *Korea Old and New*, 130–31.
81. Kim, "Korean Religious Culture and Its Affinity to Christianity," 117.
82. Buswell, *Religions of Korea*, vii–viii.
83. Buswell, *Religions of Korea*, viii.
84. Min, *Korean Religions*, vii–viii.
85. Min, *Korean Religions*, 2.
86. Koehler, *Religion in Korea*, 1.
87. Grayson, *Korea*, vii–ix.

Evil: A North Korean Christian Refugee Perspective

Grayson organized the history of Korean religious tradition into four periods of dominance: primal religion (or shamanism), Buddhist dominance, Confucian dominance, and the post-Confucian era.[88] The focus on dominance is made explicitly because, though there are periods of a singular religion in primacy, the other faiths continued to be practiced. Importantly, Grayson asserted that Korean primal religion, or shamanism, undergirds and influences all of the religious traditions that followed, up to and including modern day Christianity.[89] Additionally, Grayson noted that when Koreans do adopt a new religion, they tend to embrace the more conservative wings. This tendency seems to be somewhat paradoxical as, though Korea generally adopted conservative variations of faiths, those adoptions became syncretized with shamanism, and as such, departed from the original orthodoxy of the faith.[90]

Buswell is unique in the literature as no other source considered *Juche* as a religious or philosophical movement in the Korean peninsula.[91] Eckert et al. did not discuss the movements inside North Korea after the Korean War, while Min was limiting the research to the main, more international religious systems.[92] Grayson mentioned *Juche* as the governing philosophy of the DPRK, but otherwise did not consider it a religious movement.[93] However, as my current research is directly involving individuals who have lived in the DPRK, *Juche* as a philosophical or religious system will also need to be examined.

Another religious philosophy that must be briefly mentioned is Daoism. Daoism entered Korea at the same time as Buddhism and Confucianism.[94] Baker included it in the list of the three teachings from China that entered into Korea, although he mentioned that Daoism never achieved the same status of Buddhism or Confucianism.[95] Grayson also mentioned Daoism, but characterized it as a Chinese traditional folk religion that never took root in Korea.[96] Min omitted Daoism from the main religious

---

88. Grayson, *Korea*, 2.
89. Grayson, *Korea*, 230.
90. Grayson, *Korea*, 231.
91. Buswell, *Religions of Korea*, 1–2.
92. Min, *Korean Religions*, 1–3.
93. Grayson, *Korea*, 151.
94. Baker, *Korean Spirituality*, 54.
95. Baker, *Korean Spirituality*, 54.
96. Grayson, *Korea*, 51–52.

teachings in Korea, as did Buswell. Daoism, while enjoying a small presence in Korea, has never had an impact comparable to the other traditions, and I will not consider it as a major perspective to include.

KOREAN RELIGIOUS UNDERSTANDING OF EVIL

The main religious worldviews which influence Korean ideas about evil are shamanism, Buddhism, Confucianism, Christianity, and *Juche*. I have organized these worldviews in a manner that generally reflects the ideas therein concerning evil; specifically looking at the interplay between the degree of agency and the ontology of agency in these views.

Agency of Spiritual Beings

The belief that evil is caused by spiritual agents on some level is present in almost all forms of religion. This section, however, deals with the belief that evil is mostly due to the agency of spiritual beings. In Korean shamanism, spiritual beings are the cause of evil: People must invoke spirits to alleviate or protect them from evil. The spirits that cause evil are usually deceased relatives, although geographically local and national spirits may be blamed as well.[97]

Shamanism entered the Korean peninsula from northeast Asia in prehistoric times.[98] It can be an opaque philosophy, in that it is an oral tradition without any sacred texts. Yet it is also ubiquitous, as elements of Korean shamanism can be found all over in South Korea.[99] In the literature, shamanism can be referred to as primitive religious practices,[100] or as Korean Primal religion.[101] Whatever term is used, the subject matter is the same: the oldest extant religious beliefs in the Korean peninsula that revolve around the spirit world.

The basic belief of shamanism, according to Eckert et al., is that there are good spirits that bring good fortune upon humans, and evil spirits that bring misfortune upon humans.[102] Shamans were those people who were adept enough in magic to drive out the evil spirits and invoke the

---

97. Grayson, *Korea*, 221–25.
98. Eckert et al., *Korea Old and New*, 7.
99. Grayson, *Korea*, 230–31.
100. Eckert et al., *Korea Old and New*, 7.
101. Grayson, *Korea*, 19.
102. Eckert et al., *Korea Old and New*, 7.

good spirits. Individual or collective calamity could be avoided through the appropriate rituals being performed. The ancestor spirits in particular were believed to influence the well-being of their descendants, obligating the family to conduct ancestral worship in order to please these powerful spirits.[103] In other words, evil spirits and, if offended, ancestral spirits, were the causes of natural evil. The response to natural evil is to then perform the appropriate ceremony to appease the spirits.

The work of Eckert et al. is a general history, however, and does not delve deeply into the beliefs of shamanism. As shamanism is an oral tradition, the best analysis of the beliefs comes from examining the ritualistic songs, or *muga*. Walraven conducted such an analysis on two *muga* that had been recorded.[104] These *muga* concern the creation of the world, and the origin of suffering and death. The content of the songs gives great insight into the shamanistic perception of evil.

In the first song that Walraven analyzed, the lyrics credit the creation of the world with one specific Buddha named Maitreya.[105] This was an Edenic world without any suffering. However, a second Buddha named Sakyamuni deceived Maitreya to take dominion over the earth, and in doing so, unleashed sickness, evil spirits, suffering, and death upon the world, not unlike the Greek story of Prometheus and Pandora's box.[106]

The song is unequivocal: evil, suffering, all that is bad in the world, are due to the actions of spiritual beings. Sakyamuni unleashed the evil, and evil continues on through malevolent spirits, as the song recites:

> Maitreya, sick of being bothered by Sakyamuni, prepared to cede his age to him: "You dirty rascal Sakyamuni! If you want it to be your age, at every gat there will stand a guardian pole. If you want it to be your age, in every household dancing girls will be born, in every household there will be widows, in every household shamans will be born, in every household robbers will be born, in every household butchers will be born."[107]

The guardian poles mentioned in the song are shamanistic totems to protect from evil spirits, which were not necessary before Sakyamuni

---

103. Eckert et al., *Korea Old and New*, 22.
104. Walraven, "Creation of the World," 244–45.
105. Walraven, "Creation of the World," 246.
106. Walraven, "Creation of the World," 246.
107. Walraven, "Creation of the World," 253.

unleashed evil.¹⁰⁸ Furthermore, the song shows the degradation of humanity in morality, sickness, and power against the powers of evil spirits, thus necessitating shamans to exist in every household.

In the second song analyzed by Walraven, the origin of death is ascribed to the king of heaven and his two sons.¹⁰⁹ The older son is tricked by the younger son and is made to rule the underworld, while the younger son rules the world of humans. The interaction and deception between spiritual beings again is used to explain suffering in the world.¹¹⁰

Both songs incorporated the main religions of Korea during their time, respectively. In the first song, the Buddhas are those who are revered and in command of the spirit world.¹¹¹ In the second song, the great evil that was done was flouting the Confucian roles and hierarchy of older and younger brother.¹¹² The assimilation of other main faiths in these songs supports the assertion by Grayson that all religious faiths in Korea have been influenced by shamanism.¹¹³

While Grayson suggested that all religious traditions in Korea have been and continue to be influenced by Korean primal religion, Walraven suggested that, in actuality, it is shamanism that has been influenced by the main religions, adopting some beliefs and aspects in order to remain relevant.¹¹⁴ This may be an example of the classic chicken or egg question of causality. It is certainly beyond the scope of this current research to resolve the question; suffice it to say that in Korea, shamanism has contact with all religions. Furthermore, as Min posited, the religions in Korea have had a strong and mutual influence on each other.¹¹⁵

Bruno conducted an empirical study on another shamanistic song and ritual.¹¹⁶ Bruno observed and recorded an event when a shaman is called to usher the spirit of a deceased and decayed relative to paradise.¹¹⁷ During the ritual, the shaman prays to a variety of deities, including several

---

108. Walraven, "Creation of the World," 253.
109. Walraven, "Creation of the World," 247–48.
110. Walraven, "Creation of the World," 257–58.
111. Walraven, "Creation of the World," 246.
112. Walraven, "Creation of the World," 248.
113. Grayson, *Korea*, 230–31.
114. Walraven, "Creation of the World," 244–45.
115. Min, *Korean Religions*, 1–2.
116. Bruno, "Shamanic Ritual," 325–26.
117. Bruno, "Shamanic Ritual," 326.

Buddhas, to help carry the spirit of the deceased on to paradise.[118] If the deceased relative does not move on to paradise, unfortunate events and calamities will befall the family, which echoes the explanation given by Eckert et al. that offended ancestral spirits were the cause of evil.[119]

Additionally, the gods are invoked to protect against specific "darts" of calamities that are aimed at the family.[120] Again, the presence of elements from Buddhism and Confucianism demonstrate a degree of syncretism; practitioners pray to the Buddhas and exhort the deceased relative to become a Buddha,[121] while referring to Confucius and filial piety as well.[122] It is significant that shaman appeals to both the Buddhas and Confucius in the same song,[123] and not in different songs as the case in the songs analyzed by Walraven.[124] The song lyrics linked the gods with spreading smallpox, and implored them to refrain from spreading smallpox in that village.[125] The spirits, once again, hold the power to bring or take away calamities and sickness. Evil happens when people shirk their filial duties, or do not properly appease the gods and spirits. The gods can protect against evil but can also be the source of it.[126]

The understanding of the shamanistic view of evil was also researched by Hogarth.[127] Hogarth conducted anthropological fieldwork in Seoul over two years, interviewing and observing the practices of more than 200 shamans.[128] Using the theoretical framework of reciprocity as developed by Mauss,[129] Hogarth posited that the *kut*, or shamanist ritual, is at its core an exchange of goods between humans and spirits.[130] By inviting the spirits

---

118. Bruno, "Shamanic Ritual," 334, 349.
119. Eckert et al., *Korea Old and New*, 22.
120. Bruno, "Shamanic Ritual," 331–32.
121. Bruno, "Shamanic Ritual," 340.
122. Bruno, "Shamanic Ritual," 329, 347.
123. Bruno, "Shamanic Ritual," 340–47.
124. Walraven, "Creation of the World," 246–48.
125. Bruno, "Shamanic Ritual," 340.
126. Bruno, "Shamanic Ritual," 335–40.
127. Hogarth, "Pursuit of Happiness."
128. Hogarth, "Pursuit of Happiness," 48.
129. Mauss, *Gift*.
130. Hogarth, "Pursuit of Happiness," 58–59.

and by giving ritual offerings of food, drink, money, and entertainment, the humans obligate the spirits to reciprocate in a similar manner.[131]

Hogarth further developed the concept of reciprocity within the framework of evil or misfortune. Evil comes from the spirit world and is mitigated by appeasing the spirits. If some sort of tragedy or sickness befalls a person or family, a shaman is called to perform a *kut* and appease whatever malevolent spirit has presumably caused the tragedy or sickness.[132] While Eckert et al., Walraven, and Bruno did not utilize the theoretical framework of reciprocity explicitly, their understanding of the shamanistic perception of evil is in line with Hogarth.

One additional interesting point that Hogarth made is regarding Korean ethnic nationalism. There is a plethora of spirits in the Korean shamanistic pantheon, and there are also several specific human-gods, Korean national heroes of the past who can be called upon to aid Koreans in the present.[133] Korean nationalism is also present in the ceremony and song described by Bruno.[134] The marriage of shamanism and nationalism in this worldview may prove significant in regard to North Korean Christians' perceptions of evil.

The shamanist view of evil, then, is entirely based upon the agency of spiritual beings. It is the spiritual forces who bring calamity and sickness, and it is those same spiritual forces who need to be appealed to in order to alleviate suffering. While I have only focused on the way shamanism attributes evil to spiritual agency, there are, as was noted, certainly aspects of Buddhism and Confucianism at play in the shamanistic worldview, particularly in which spirits to revere and the idea of morality.

Agency of Human Beings

This section examines sources which discuss the way human agents are responsible for evil. The literature here represents the combined avowed belief systems of many people on the Korean peninsula today.

There are three different religious or philosophical perspectives included here; Confucian, Christian, and *Juche* ideology. The three different viewpoints vary in the degree to which they hold human agents as responsible,

131. Hogarth, "Pursuit of Happiness," 64.
132. Hogarth, "Pursuit of Happiness," 49–50.
133. Hogarth, "Pursuit of Happiness," 52–54.
134. Bruno, "Shamanic Ritual," 327–28.

and the literature reflects different degrees of human responsibility within the Confucian, Christian, and *Juche* schools of thought as well.

In the next section, I will show that *Juche* places complete responsibility for evil on human agents, which is generally defined as disloyalty to the *Juche* system. Confucian thought places a great deal of responsibility of evil on human agents who fail in maintaining their proper role in society, which can upset the delicate balance of the universe and cause evil to befall. Note that Confucian literature debates whether humans are innately evil or innately good. Christianity shows the greatest theological spectrum in regards to evil and human agency, with some sources placing a heavy emphasis on the spiritual agents in the cause of evil as well. However, all of the Christian sources still place the responsibility of evil upon human agents.

Confucian views of evil

Confucianism as a philosophy and religion entered the Korean peninsula around the fourth century AD from China, but the National Confucian College was not established until AD 682.[135] Buddhism was the dominant religion up until the adoption of Confucianism as the form of spirituality preferred by the royalty and ruling class during the Joseon dynasty.[136] In fact, the era of Confucianism as the dominant religion in Korea lasted almost the entire length of the Joseon dynasty, from about the fourteenth to nineteenth centuries.[137]

Confucianism assumes that if relationships are properly maintained, then conflict will be minimized and social harmony will prevail.[138] There are five key relationships that need to be harmonious in the Confucian worldview: the relationships between husband and wife, father and son, elder brother and younger brother, ruler and ruled, and friend to friend.[139]

Baker explained that in Korea, Confucianists saw the universe as a thing in balance. When disaster struck, such as a flood or a bad storm, the cause was the imbalance in nature due to individuals not adequately fulfilling their appropriate Confucian roles as a father, wife, son, etc. The cause of evil, both natural and social, is directly related to human actions,

---

135. Eckert et al., *Korea Old and New*, 52.
136. Baker, *Korean Spirituality*, 33, 46.
137. Grayson, *Korea*, 112–36.
138. Baker, *Korean Spirituality*, 45.
139. Baker, *Korean Spirituality*, 42.

Literature Review

and the remedy of evil has to do with a re-invigorated pursuit of Confucian social harmony.[140]

Kim conducted an examination of Confucian social hierarchy during the Joseon dynasty.[141] In this article, Kim examined the Korean Joseon dynasty's rulings regarding vengeance murders and filial piety.[142] While Kim discussed several different cases of revenge murders committed by children on their fathers' murders, one case in particular that occurred in 1795 is discussed at length, involving a married daughter who took vengeance on her father's murderer.[143]

In the Confucian teaching, the highest loyalty and duty is to one's parents. In the case of a married woman, however, her loyalty is supposed to be transferred to her husband's parents.[144] In this particular case the woman was married, and as such should perhaps not have avenged her father's death; however, she did, and she was acquitted by the Confucian courts, as it was viewed as a highly moral thing to do.[145] On the contrary, the wife of the man she killed fled the scene, presumably to save her own life, and she was charged by the court for failing to remain with her husband.[146]

Kim's example of a vengeance killing highlights the importance of the Confucian relationship structure in Korean society, including in the concepts of morality and legality. The demonstration of filial piety, even in the act of a vengeance killing, was not only considered moral, but considered to be good and worthy of replication. While some concepts of morality would place a higher value on a person's life than on vengeance, Korean Confucianism does not necessarily follow the same logic. In Korean Confucianism, filial piety trumps all, and playing the proper role in relationships is tantamount to goodness; as a corollary, evil would be the shirking of one's filial duties. The understanding that Kim expressed regarding good and evil as viewed by the Korean Confucianists echoed what Baker wrote earlier: Confucianists evaluate good and evil on the basis of social duties and relationships.[147]

---

140. Baker, *Korean Spirituality*, 48–53.
141. Kim, "Between Morality and Crime," 481.
142. Kim, "Between Morality and Crime," 482.
143. Kim, "Between Morality and Crime," 482.
144. Kim, "Between Morality and Crime," 497.
145. Kim, "Between Morality and Crime," 496.
146. Kim, "Between Morality and Crime," 497–98.
147. Kim, "Between Morality and Crime," 496–98.

Evil: A North Korean Christian Refugee Perspective

Confucianism as a school of thought is not monolithic, however, specifically in regard to the nature of humans. As a philosopher, Perrett established three distinct positions about the relationship between human nature and evil: optimism, pessimism, and dualism.[148] Optimism posits that human nature is basically good, pessimism posits that human nature is basically evil, and dualism posits that human nature is both good and evil.

Perrett then used these distinct positions as a lens to examine the assertions regarding human nature and evil from two of Confucius' disciples, Mencius and Xunzi.[149] Mencius argued that human nature is basically good, and that evil comes as humans are corrupted by society and culture. The cause of evil is poor social order, with the remedy being a properly ordered society.[150] This explanation is in line with the understanding of Confucianism as explained by Baker.[151]

Xunzi disagreed with Mencius, and argued that human nature was basically evil and that humans needed to be taught how to be good.[152] The cause of evil is human nature, and the remedy is, just as Mencius argued, education and a properly ordered society. Xunzi's position sounds somewhat similar to idea behind the "re-education" camps found in communist countries, including North Korea.[153] However, Mencius' position has been historically the dominant school of thought in Confucianism, asserting that human nature is basically good.

JUCHE VIEWS OF EVIL

Juche, the official ideology of North Korea, was created recently, although the exact origins and development of *Juche* ideology are debated. Some scholars assert it began with Kim Il Sung in 1955,[154] while others argue that it was not until the 1960s that it was developed and propagated.[155] Regardless of the exact starting date and the period of development, it is clear that *Juche* was, at least to the outside world, the official ideology of

---

148. Perrett, "Evil and Human Nature," 309.
149. Perrett, "Evil and Human Nature," 312.
150. Perrett, "Evil and Human Nature," 312–13.
151. Baker, *Korean Spirituality*, 48–53.
152. Perrett, "Evil and Human Nature," 315.
153. See Kang and Rigoulot, *Aquariums of Pyeongyang*.
154. Belke, *Juche*, 173–75.
155. Myers, *Juche Myth*, 93–97.

North Korea by the early 1970s.[156] Later expanded upon by Kim Il Sung's son and heir, Kim Jong Il, *Juche* is an ideology that claims to be a continuation of Marxist-Leninist political theory that has been appropriately adapted and enhanced for the Korean context.[157]

Juche is asserted to be the culmination of philosophical thought and the pathway towards ultimate human flourishing.[158] The messianic undertones of the *Juche* ideology are impossible to ignore, leaving *Juche*, a proclaimed atheistic ideology, seemingly a religious system.[159] In particular, the cult of personality surrounding Kim Il Sung and Kim Jong Il comes across as, at the very least, ancestor veneration, bordering on monarch deification.

There are two main causes of evil in the *Juche* worldview: disloyalty to the *Juche* system, and disloyalty to the Korean race. These two causes of evil are developed in the literature surrounding *Juche*.

The seminal work is Kim Jong Il's treatise on *Juche*.[160] In this work, Kim put forth his world view according to the *Juche* ideology.

> The idea that man is the master of everything and decides everything, in other words, the idea that man is the master of the world and his own destiny and is the transformer of the world and the shaper of his destiny, is fundamentally opposed to idealism and metaphysics. Idealism leads to mystical theory that the world and man's destiny are controlled by the supernatural "might," while metaphysics leads to the fatalistic belief that everything in the world is immutable and, accordingly, man must be obedient to his predetermined destiny. The idea that man is the master of the world and his own destiny and is able to transform the world and shape his destiny, is based on the premise of the materialistic and dialectical viewpoint which denies mysticism and fatalism.[161]

This worldview is completely materialistic and humanistic, denying any type of spiritual or supernatural existence. Evil is placed purely in the hands of the individual, whose actions are deemed good if they are done in accordance with the leader's commands, which are meant for the guidance of the nation, and evil if the individual looks elsewhere for guidance.

156. Myers, *Juche Myth*, 119–22.
157. Kim, *On the Juche Idea*.
158. Kim, *On the Juche Idea*, 62.
159. Belke, *Juche*, 79.
160. Kim, *On the Juche Idea*.
161. Kim, *On the Juche Idea*, 60.

Evil: A North Korean Christian Refugee Perspective

> The nationalists and self-styled Marxists followed the evil practices of flunkeyism and factional strife which had resulted in the country's ruin in the past. They did not try to carry out the revolution by their own initiative but dreamed of achieving independence by depending on foreign forces.[162]

Evil is specifically associated in this text with flunkeyism and the influence of foreign powers, as opposed to a purely Korean revolution.

Belke's study on *Juche* is one of the most complete works on approaching the *Juche* worldview as a state religion.[163] While the book relied heavily on primary sources from the DPRK, Belke's own style of citation offers little opportunity for further research on the source material. Regardless, the work brought an important and distinctively Christian lens to the examination of *Juche*, including the morality system inherent within.

Juche, according to Belke, is philosophically very similar to humanism, with a cult of personality included. In the *Juche* system, failing to worship the leader can result in evil.[164] Disloyalty is treated harshly, and the leader is the ultimate arbitrator of what is evil and what is good.[165] In the *Juche* ideology, the leader is not blamed for natural disasters; the oppression of outside states that are opposed to the *Juche* system are responsible for disasters.[166] While Belke himself believed evil, specifically in the North Korean context, as demonically and spiritually charged,[167] the human-centered nature of *Juche* lays the responsibility of evil upon individuals who do not live up to the proper standards of the *Juche* ideology.

Cho made a comparison between *Juche*, Christianity, and the Korean Christian liberation theology, known as Minjung theology.[168] By comparing the views of these three worldviews on their assertions regarding humanity, humans, history, and the future, Cho was able to clearly distinguish areas of connection and areas of division. Specifically, in regard to evil, Cho highlighted that in *Juche* all morality is based on loyalty to the leader.[169] While there is denial of sin or sin nature in *Juche*, disloyalty is viewed as

---

162. Kim, *On the Juche Idea*, 6.
163. Belke, *Juche*, 1–2.
164. Belke, *Juche*, 13–18.
165. Belke, *Juche*, 24.
166. Belke, *Juche*, 9–10.
167. Belke, *Juche*, 80–83.
168. Cho, "Encounter," 82–83.
169. Cho, "Encounter," 85.

Literature Review

evil. The future utopia would be a society where everyone has become *Juche* humans in perfect loyalty to the leader.[170] Cho and Belke agree regarding the question of evil in the *Juche* worldview.

The DPRK has an official list of ideological principles called the Ten Principles of Life.[171] These principles, meant to guide DPRK citizens, were originally written under Kim Il Sung. The principles are:

1. All societies [the whole world] must be governed by the Great Leader's ideologies.
2. The Great Leader must be revered and adored.
3. The authority of the Great Leader is absolute.
4. The ideology and principles of the Great Leader must be the guiding principles of the actions and thoughts of all.
5. Execute the directives of the Great Leader without any questions.
6. Unite and rally all people around the Great Leader.
7. Learn from the Great Leader, his moral character, and strategic planning for the future.
8. Repay the Great Leader's trust in and care for the people through the successful implementation of his vision.
9. Establish stringent organizational rules that follow only the Great Leader's directives.
10. Continue the revolutionary struggles in accordance with the achievements of the Great Leader, and by the succession of his family line forever.[172]

While this list may seem more like 10 principles to enforce totalitarianism, they demand the ideological loyalty of the people. Evil would be anything that is contrary to the ten principles; indeed, during the weekly self and group criticizing sessions in North Korea, others are accused of falling short of living out these ten principles.[173] Similar to the Judeo-Christian adherence to the Ten Commandments as prescribed in the Bible, the 10 principles present a moral guidepost or yardstick to North Koreans. In

---

170. Cho, "Encounter," 93–94.
171. Kim et al., *Reflections*, 23.
172. Kim et al., *Reflections*, 23.
173. See Holmes and Hong, "Contextualization of the Gospel."

fact, the 10 principles are sometimes referred to as the 10 commandments of North Korea.[174]

Enshrined in the 10 principles is the *Juche* concept of the *Suryong*, or great leader.[175] The concept of the *Suryong* is explained using a human body metaphor. The *Suryong* is the head and brain of the body, and the party and ideology are like the blood that carries oxygen to the muscles, which are symbolic of the masses.[176]

Stated otherwise, "The Great Leader is the brain that makes decisions and issues orders, the Party is the nervous system that channels information, and the people are the bone and muscle that physically execute the orders."[177] Using this analogy, without the leader the masses would be aimless and the "body" would cease to be alive. In addition to the title of Eternal *Suryong*, Kim Il Sung is often referred to as "father," which carries a significance of loyalty, love, and authority, especially in a culture with Confucianist roots.[178]

The very idea of life is developed uniquely in *Juche* as well. *Juche* ideology teaches that there are two types of life: physical life which is temporal and ends definitively, and sociopolitical life that can be eternal.[179] The sociopolitical life, which is realized in the individual faithfully working to support the political system, is considered eternal because the efforts of the individual continue to be significant if the political system continues.[180] Sociopolitical life is tied to the *Suryong*, who ensures the survival of the political system. Thus, loyalty to the *Suryong* is akin to eternal political life, while disloyalty to the *Suryong* means the end of both physical and political life. Evil, to put it simply, is disloyalty to the leader.

There is an alternative perspective concerning *Juche* in the literature. Myers is an avid scholar and researcher who holds the dissenting voice in the discussion of the DPRK and the *Juche* worldview. Myers identified three tracks of North Korean propaganda; one external track targeted for outsiders, one middle track targeted for internal use but which may be observed by

174. Kim et al., *Reflections*, 23.
175. Belke, *Juche*, 22.
176. Cho, "Encounter," 96.
177. Lee, "Political Philosophy of Juche," 111.
178. Belke, *Juche*, 56.
179. Cho, "Encounter," 87.
180. Cho, "Encounter," 87.

Literature Review

outsiders, and one that is meant for an internal audience only.[181] Through his analysis of the propaganda, Myers rejected the notion that Confucianism, Buddhism, Christianity, or shamanism have any influence in the worldview of North Korea. Myers asserted that North Korea is actually guided by a militant race-based nationalism; the greatest crime of all would be betrayal of the race.[182] The Korean race, according to Myers' interpretation of the North Korean worldview, is inherently virtuous and good, and needs to be protected from the corrupt and evil outside world.[183]

Myers wrote as a scholar who researches and teaches in South Korea, giving him a unique perspective in approaching issues regarding the Korean peninsula. While simultaneously treating the DPRK with utmost seriousness and with some contempt, Myers' argument regarding the North Korean worldview is backed by his research.

In his more recent work, Myers directly approached the *Juche* worldview and defined it as merely a myth.[184] Again, as in his previous work, Myers conducted an analysis of the internal and external propaganda present in the DPRK, along with primary source research involving the seminal speeches and works that launched *Juche*.[185] Myers' argument was that the DPRK developed and promoted *Juche* only for outside nations to take the DPRK seriously on the world stage as an innovator of its own ideology, not simply adopting Soviet-style communism.[186] In actuality, according to Myers, the ideology of the DPRK is race-based nationalism, which the ruling class knows is not an ideology that is acceptable on the global stage.[187] *Juche*, Myers asserted, has no bearing on the domestic or foreign policies of the DPRK.[188]

Myers did concede that the *Juche* ideology has greatly assisted the development of the cult of personality surrounding the Kim family, but did not believe that *Juche* itself as an ideology has much influence on the daily life of North Koreans.[189] Myers' work is important to include, as it is a dissenting

181. Myers, *Juche Myth*, 11–13.
182. Myers, *Cleanest Race*, 8–11.
183. Myers, *Cleanest Race*, 9.
184. Myers, *Juche Myth*, 2–3.
185. Myers, *Juche Myth*, 9.
186. Myers, *Juche Myth*, 6.
187. Myers, *Juche Myth*, 3.
188. Myers, *Juche Myth*, 3.
189. Myers, *Juche Myth*, 2–3.

Evil: A North Korean Christian Refugee Perspective

voice that did not express a belief that *Juche* as an ideology has much meaning at all on the Korean peninsula, in regards to evil or philosophical thought. This is in contrast to Belke,[190] Cho,[191] and Kang,[192] who all argued that *Juche* has an ever-present influence on daily life in North Korea.

Myers does have an ally in Kang in one regard, as someone who argued that the DPRK holds ethno-nationalism and the rejection of foreigner intervention as paramount.[193] Good, then, is self-reliance and the ability to avoid any foreign influence.

Kang noted that *Juche* explicitly denies any outside force, such as fate, as having any bearing on the world.[194] Humans are the subject and the master of all reality. Evil, then, has to do only with human actions, the oppression of the Korean people by foreigners, and anything that damages or risks the self-reliance of the nation.

CHRISTIAN PERSPECTIVES OF EVIL

Christianity also provides perspectives on evil and suffering in Korea. In the following section I will discuss how the advent of Christianity in Korea resulted in tremendous suffering for the converts. Then I will discuss how Christianity has provided a lens for understanding these evils.

PERSECUTION OF CHRISTIANS IN KOREA

While scholars debate if Nestorian missionaries who traveled East ever made it as far as Korea, the first priest recorded to enter Korea actually came as a chaplain to an invading Japanese army during the reign of Hideyoshi.[195] Father Gregorio de Cespedes, a Jesuit, spent several months in Korea attached to a Japanese garrison.[196] He was sent back to Japan after several months due to some disagreements with Buddhist Japanese generals.[197] While in Korea, he was not able to preach or communicate with the Korean

---

190. Belke, *Juche*, 3.
191. Cho, "Encounter," 96–97.
192. Kang, "Lens of *Juche*," 43.
193. Kang, "Lens of *Juche*," 45.
194. Kang, "Lens of *Juche*," 43.
195. Kim, *History of Christianity in Korea*, 29.
196. Kim, *History of Christianity in Korea*, 29.
197. Kim, *History of Christianity in Korea*, 31.

people, as he was unable to speak Korean and attached to an invading force. Nevertheless, he is the first known Catholic priest to enter Korea.

The first Korean converts to Christianity came by way of the educated class's annual trips to China. These scholars met with foreigners at the court in China, including several Catholic priests.[198] Through discussions and reading books, several of the educated class brought back basic Christian belief and practices, which began to spread among the scholars.[199] The first Catholic church was established in 1784,[200] and by 1795 there were an estimated four thousand Catholic believers inside Korea.[201]

Persecution against the church began almost immediately as the church began to grow.[202] The initial growth of the Catholic church was, in some sense, planted and watered by the blood of the Catholic martyrs in Korea.[203] The persecution against Christians began almost from the beginning of the first established Catholic churches. At its core, Korea is a culture based on a Confucian ideology. Christianity threatened that ideology by Christians refusing to take part in the traditional ancestor veneration, and by proclaiming that all were equal before God, a clear affront to the hierarchy of the Confucian system.[204]

Yun Ji Chung, a Catholic convert, became the center of the religious controversy when, in 1791, he not only refused to conduct the ancestral veneration rites on the death of his mother, but he additionally burnt all of his family's veneration tablets.[205] Yun was arrested and,

> although he could have recanted and been released, under interrogation and torture Yun continued to declare that ancestor veneration was a sin against the Lord and was forbidden by the Catholic Church. He used Catholic arguments to criticize the Confucian custom as idolatrous worship of wooden tablets and even flatly contradicted Confucian doctrine by insisting that loyalty and filial piety were not absolute but were based on the law of God.[206]

---

198. Kim, *History of Christianity in Korea*, 36–38.
199. Kim, *History of Christianity in Korea*, 38.
200. Adams, "Church Growth in Korea," 3.
201. Eckert et al., *Korea Old and New*, 171.
202. Adams, "Church Growth in Korea," 3.
203. Kim, *History of Christianity in Korea*, 63.
204. Adams, "Church Growth in Korea," 3.
205. Kim, *History of Christianity in Korea*, 27.
206. Kim, *History of Christianity in Korea*, 27.

Yun was beheaded, along with his cousin, and his extended family was sent into exile or enslaved as further punishment for his crime.[207]

Adams stated:

> Thus, the first century of the Catholic Church in Korea was characterized by a series of persecutions in which thousands died. It is estimated that between 1801 and 1876 over 10,000 Catholics were executed because of their refusal to follow the traditional Confucian ancestral rites. The Church was therefore placed in a position of opposition to the royal court. Catholics were forced to live in isolated rural villages, sometimes deep in the mountains, and they were unable to found any institutions such as schools, universities, or hospitals. The Church played no official role in Korean cultural life, and in the latter years of the Chosun Dynasty when some Neo-Confucian scholars became influenced by Catholic ideas, and in several instances even became converts, these scholars were either executed or sent into exile.[208]

The treatment of the Catholics in this period of time fluctuated between aggressive persecution and tacit acceptance, largely depending on who was wielding the political power,[209] which affirms the postulations of Min that the main faiths experienced exclusion or persecution, accommodation, and assimilation.[210] Internal fighting between political factions saw Catholicism being used as a tool to attack rivals when the time was right.[211]

Foreign missionaries secretly entered the country during the 1800s to undertake the work of ministry to the believers.[212] These mainly French priests operated clandestinely. They, however, were not spared in the seasons of persecution; nine of the twelve foreign priests were beheaded, with the remaining three priests fleeing Korea.[213]

Korea closed its borders to the outside world in the mid 1800s, only to have them forced open in the 1880s when the foreign powers arrived with gun ships and began signing trade treaties with Korea.[214] At this

---

207. Kim, *History of Christianity in Korea*, 27.
208. Adams, "Church Growth in Korea," 3.
209. Kim, *History of Christianity in Korea*, 54–55.
210. Min, *Korean Religions*, 2.
211. Kim, *History of Christianity in Korea*, 55.
212. Kim, *History of Christianity in Korea*, 64–65.
213. Kim, *History of Christianity in Korea*, 46.
214. Kim, *History of Christianity in Korea*, 113–15.

time, the Catholic church, which had been under duress since its arrival, finally received relief, as the foreign powers ensured the safety of Christians in Korea.

To summarize, Catholicism was initially brought to Korea by Koreans who had learned of it while in China. The educated class embraced this new teaching, but its existence was subject to the whims of whoever was in power at a given time. Christianity was outlawed by royal edict, and Christians were sought out, tortured, and executed.

Protestants, mainly the Presbyterians and Methodists, began to plant churches in Korea in the late nineteenth century.[215] As the early Protestant missionaries entered Korea through China, the Protestant churches were concentrated in the northern areas of the Korean peninsula.[216] In 1907 a great revival broke out in Pyeongyang, earning it the nickname "the Jerusalem of the East."[217]

The Empire of Japan formally annexed Korea in 1910. What followed was a concerted effort to stomp out Korean culture and anything that was viewed as anti-Japanese, Christianity included.[218] The assignment as "anti-Japanese" by the oppressor strengthened the standing of Christianity among the populace.[219] The church in Korea, both in the North and the South, suffered under Japanese persecution. After the surrender of Japan at the end of World War II, however, the Christians in the North would suffer additional persecutions. Pyeongyang, which had once been the center of Christianity in Korea, was now firmly controlled by the Soviet-backed communist forces.[220]

Following the outbreak of the Korean War in 1950, more than one million refugees, many of them Christians, fled from the Northern controlled Communist Korea to the South.[221] Thus, Christians in both the North and South of Korean peninsula have a shared heritage and experience in the recent past. Christianity, far from being considered a foreign faith, was firmly established in the entirety of the peninsula long before the Korean War split the peninsula in two.

215. Kim, *History of Christianity in Korea*, 129–31.
216. Kim, *History of Christianity in Korea*, 122–31.
217. Kim, *History of Christianity in Korea*, 83.
218. Kim, *History of Christianity in Korea*, 114–19.
219. Kim, *History of Christianity in Korea*, 203.
220. Kim, *History of Christianity in Korea*, 438–39.
221. Chung, "Reflection," 326.

Evil: A North Korean Christian Refugee Perspective

CHRISTIAN LITERATURE ON EVIL

The Christian literature on evil is the most thoroughly developed of all the worldviews found in the Korean peninsula. This may be because, as C. S. Lewis argued, pain and evil are not a problem to be solved unless one believes in an omnipotent and good God.[222] Theologians from all backgrounds have argued their perspectives regarding evil and the Christian worldview. It would be impossible to exhaustively cover the literature for these perspectives. However, as there are a number of competing views regarding evil in Christianity, I will attempt to select some key writings from a variety of theological backgrounds to serve as a larger sample of the Christian perspective of evil. In particular, I will examine the difference from the Calvinist and the Arminian perspectives on evil, as representative of the theological understanding of the two main Protestant denominations that entered Korea: Presbyterians, or Reform, adhering to Calvinistic beliefs, while Methodists adhere to Arminian beliefs. I will additionally examine how Christians in Korea have historically expressed their understanding of evil. Finally, I will briefly examine more recent, alternative, views of evil that do not fit in the above-mentioned categories.

Arminian Beliefs on Evil

One of the more famous works from a Christian perspective comes from philosopher Plantinga.[223] Plantinga directly addressed the problem of evil as put forth by atheist philosopher Mackie.[224] Mackie stated that there is a logical contradiction in believing that a good God exists and is omnipotent.[225] Plantinga, who came from a Reform Christian background, effectively argued a free-will defense to the problem of evil. In his defense, Plantinga argued that God made individuals in the world as genuinely free, meaning that individuals are capable of being morally good, but must be capable of being morally corrupt as well.[226]

Plantinga essentially placed the responsibility of evil at the hands of genuinely free creatures (which includes humans and spiritual beings).

---

222. Lewis, *Problem of Pain*.
223. Plantinga, *God, Freedom, and Evil*.
224. Plantinga, *God, Freedom, and Evil*, 12.
225. Mackie, "Evil and Omnipotence," 200.
226. Plantinga, *God, Freedom, and Evil*, 29–32.

It would be impossible, Plantinga argued, for God to create a world in which creatures are genuinely free that would not contain the possibility of evil.[227] The responsibility of evil is on the agency as exercised by the genuinely free creatures, when it is expressed in contradiction to what God has decreed is good.

This is seminal work in Christian theology and philosophy regarding the nature of evil. Plantinga is often cited by subsequent authors, and his work continues to be relevant to this day.[228] Notably, in contrast to Boyd, Plantinga did not offer a theodicy proper, but rather a defense, which he distinguished by the former asserting why God permits evil, and the latter proposing one possible reason that God permits evil.[229]

Boyd built on Plantinga, and developed a deeper theological perspective.[230] In this work, Boyd addressed what he terms as the "blueprint theology" that was handed down by St. Augustine, and posited a different theodicy based on what Boyd referred to as a "trinitarian warfare" worldview.[231] Boyd rejected the notion that everything that happens "somehow fits into God's secret plan—a divine blueprint."[232] Boyd identified St. Augustine and John Calvin as the originator and propagator, respectively, of this idea, and reached back into early church writings to argue that Christians before Augustine did not adhere to such an extreme view of providence.[233]

Boyd's work on the Christian view of evil is similar to Plantinga's but went further in its assertions. Boyd argued that instead of simply the responsibility of the evil actions being ascribed to the agency of the actors, the ultimate reason of the evil actions should be ascribed to the actors as well, and not to God. Natural evil, Boyd argued, can be understood as proof that the world exists in a state of warfare between God and those that oppose God.[234]

In his other works, Boyd established the nature of the spiritual state of warfare in the world, and later posited that Christian views of evil must

---

227. Plantinga, *God, Freedom, and Evil*, 31.

228. See further: Alcorn, *If God Is Good*; Boyd, *Satan and the Problem of Evil*; Thweatt-Bates, "Chaos and the Problem of Evil."

229. Plantinga, *God, Freedom, and Evil*, 28.

230. Boyd, *Satan and the Problem of Evil*.

231. Boyd, *Satan and the Problem of Evil*, 16.

232. Boyd, *Satan and the Problem of Evil*, 13–18.

233. Boyd, *Satan and the Problem of Evil*, 12–13.

234. Boyd, *Satan and the Problem of Evil*, 20.

include an idea of divine aikido.[235] Aikido is a martial art that is defensive in nature, and only returns the attacker's force back upon the attacker. Divine aikido, according to Boyd is the idea that God does not cause evil, but can withdraw his ever-present protection to allow the repercussions of evil to affect the perpetrators.[236]

While Boyd built on the work of Plantinga, Plantinga wrote from a Reformed Christian perspective, whereas Boyd identified himself as writing from the Christian perspective from the other end of the theological spectrum which espouses Arminianism, and, at the extreme, open-theism.[237]

Calvinist Views on Evil

Opposite of Boyd on the theological spectrum is Alcorn. Alcorn wrote great lengths to identify potential questions that individuals might have when wrestling with the problem of evil, and offered a variety of explanations from across the Christian spectrum.[238] Alcorn identified primary evil, which is a moral choice to go against God, and secondary evil, which is the consequences of the primary evil that humans experience.[239] As a result of the fall, the world is under a curse and experiences natural disasters and other hardships, which Alcorn defined as secondary evils. According to Alcorn, in Christianity, God allows and sometimes determines secondary evils to occur, but the responsibility of the primary and secondary evil is the agency of individuals.[240] The determination of the secondary evil is sometimes God-ordained.

Alcorn asserted that sometimes suffering is inflicted for a higher good that humans cannot see, similar to the description that Boyd gave of the blueprint theology.[241] While his own view on evil seems to be a synthesis of human agency and divine sovereignty, Alcorn took specific issue with Boyd's understanding of evil.[242] Alcorn asserted that Boyd's understanding of God and the reality of evil show a diminished view of God's omniscience.

235. Boyd, *God at War*, 13.
236. Boyd, *Crucifixion of the Warrior God*, 768–69.
237. Boyd, *God at War*, 87.
238. Alcorn, *If God Is Good*, 1–5.
239. Alcorn, *If God Is Good*, 26–29.
240. Alcorn, *If God Is Good*, 26–27.
241. Alcorn, *If God Is Good*, 392–96.
242. Alcorn, *If God Is Good*, 146–47.

While Boyd's theodicy does not necessitate an acceptance of open theism, Alcorn conflated open theism and Boyd's theodicy, and attacked the theological concept of open theism itself.[243] According to Alcorn, open theism is theologically incorrect, not backed by the Bible, and offers a shallow answer to the problem of evil. However, Boyd stated that open theism is not a prerequisite to his theodicy postulations; rather, his view of evil is grounded in mainstream Arminian theology.[244]

The main distinction that emerges from the literature between the Reformed or Calvinist viewpoint and the Arminian viewpoint is that of causality. Secondary evil, as described by Alcorn can be attributed to God in the former viewpoint, but is not attributed to God in the latter. Boyd's postulation of divine aikido stands in contrast to Alcorn's views on secondary evil.

Korean Christian Views on Evil

The understanding that Korean Christians had regarding evil was examined in historical research conducted by Rausch. Rausch reviewed the writings of six Korean Christians from the late 18th century through the twentieth century in order to understand the writers' theodicies.[245] One writer examined by Rausch was Catholic theologian Augustine Chong Yak-Chong.

Augustine Chong Yak-Chong wrote a catechism in the 1790s in which he addressed the problem of evil

> by stressing that this ultimate reckoning did not take place until after death. Augustine explained that God waits until human beings die to punish them to provide them time to repent of their actions. . . . Augustine's theodicy focused on an afterlife, as it was only in eternity that the good could be sufficiently rewarded and the evil adequately punished.[246]

Thus, the understanding of evil and theodicy, according to Augustine Chong Yak-Chong, only made sense when viewed teleologically. Beyond theodicy, Augustine Chong Yak-Chong also addressed the nature of evil

---

243. Alcorn, *If God Is Good*, 146–47.
244. Boyd, *God at War*, 86–87.
245. Rausch, "Suffering History," 70.
246. Rausch, "Suffering History," 72.

and wrote that evil was not anything God did, but rather because of the free choice of Adam and Eve to sin, which has led to evil and suffering.[247]

Augustine Chong Yak-Chong was martyred in 1801,[248] and his nephew, Alexander Sayong Hwang, fled and wrote a famous letter on a piece of silk to the bishop of Beijing pleading for help from foreign governments to end the persecution of Catholics in Korea.[249] Hwang's letter was found by the government authorities and led to his execution, and was used later in the process of Hwang's canonization as a Catholic saint.[250] In the content of the silk letter Hwang revealed his belief that the persecution the church was suffering was divine punishment for its ingratitude.[251]

> The Lord's grace arrived in Korea in an extraordinary way. No missionaries brought Catholic teachings to Korea. Instead, the Lord himself implanted Catholicism here. After that, He bestowed His grace upon us through the sacraments, and so we have enjoyed more special blessings than we could ever count. The punishment we have suffered this year from persecution is because of our lack of gratitude for these blessings.[252]

The understanding of the source and nature of the suffering of the church that Hwang believed laid the responsibility of suffering with the specific sins of the contemporaneous church, while holding God as the punisher. Hwang takes a more direct cause and effect understanding of suffering than Augustine Chong Yak-Chong professed, and echoes the belief that the North Korean theologians expressed that they had been told from South Koreans as reported by Yoo.[253] Hwang's position is in line with that explained by Alcorn, that this suffering is intended for a higher purpose, and that God is responsible for the secondary evil.[254]

A third Korean Christian view understanding of evil was put forth by Thomas An Chunggun during the period of the Japanese occupation of Korea.[255] Thomas is famous for the assassination of the Japanese prime

247. Rausch, "Suffering History," 72–73.
248. Rausch, "Suffering History," 74.
249. Hwang and Kim, "Silk Letter," 165.
250. Hwang and Kim, "Silk Letter," 167.
251. Rausch, "Suffering History," 76.
252. Baker and Rausch, *Catholics in Korea*, 195.
253. Yoo, *Learning Experiences*, 280.
254. Alcorn, *If God Is Good*, 342–51.
255. Rausch, "Suffering History," 77.

minister, Ito Hirobumi.[256] Thomas was a Catholic nationalist, and combined the Korean nationalist struggle with Catholicism, and doing so, found a scapegoat for the evil and suffering that the Korean people were suffering.

> Thomas moved away from ascribing the suffering experienced by the Korean nation to any personal sin among them or even to original sin. Instead, he blamed Korea's suffering on the actions of one man: Ito Hirobumi.[257]

Thomas was so convinced in his beliefs that he assassinated Ito Hirobumi, and was later executed as a criminal.[258] Thomas' belief of the cause of evil moved from the sin of the church and consequent punishment from God, as held by Hwang, to the sin of one foreign man.

A progression can be seen in this brief glimpse of the historical Korean Christian understandings of evil. Augustine Chong Yak-Chong understood evil teleologically, and held Adam and Eve's original sin to be the cause of current evil.[259] Hwang understood evil to be the punishment of God on an ungrateful and sinful church.[260] Thomas understood evil to be caused by one sinful man, Ito Hirobumi, and did not hold God responsible for the suffering that he and the Korean nation experienced.[261]

Additional Christian Views on Evil

Theologian N. T. Wright furthered the discussion of evil from a Christian perspective.[262] Wright highlighted the difference between moral evil and natural evil, and traced the main discussion of evil from a Christian standpoint from the Lisbon earthquake of 1755.[263] While discussing evil in a serious and thoughtful manner, Wright did not take a bold stand regarding the nature of evil like Boyd and Alcorn did. Instead, Wright believed Christianity offers a teleological answer to evil, and suggested that while humans cannot understand evil now, people can know that one day

---

256. Rausch, "Suffering History," 77.
257. Rausch, "Suffering History," 80.
258. Rausch, "Suffering History," 80.
259. Rausch, "Suffering History," 72.
260. Rausch, "Suffering History," 75–76.
261. Rausch, "Suffering History," 78.
262. Wright, *Evil and the Justice of God*.
263. Wright, *Evil and the Justice of God*, 19–21, 103.

Evil: A North Korean Christian Refugee Perspective

all shall be well, and God's justice will be done to evil.[264] While different from the position of Augustine Chong Yak-Chong,[265] both Wright and Augustine Chong Yak-Chong believed that evil can only be understood through a teleological lens.

Another theologian, Cornelius Plantinga discussed evil from the lens of sin.[266] In his theological review of sin, Plantinga defined evil as "any spoiling of shalom, whether physically (e.g., by disease), morally, spiritually or otherwise."[267] Plantinga then discussed moral and spiritual evil as requiring agents and actions or dispositions.[268]

Central to Plantinga's understanding of evil is his postulation of the "Great Law of Returns,"[269] through which he explained why evil exists:

> The reason is that, generally speaking, you reap what you sow. This is simply how things are in the universe. There is no explaining it, no use railing against it, usually no way to get around it. We might as well as try to get around the law of gravity. We might as well argue with our body's need for sleep.[270]

While echoing his brother Alvin Plantinga's emphasis on choices leading to sin, Plantinga also discussed the interplay between personal and societal culpability in sin, but concluded that only God knows to what extent evil is due to agents or due to environments.

A different interesting viewpoint from a Christian perspective was put forth by Thweatt-Bates.[271] In this fascinating article, Thweatt-Bates utilized the emerging concept of chaos theory, used in a number of physical and social sciences and applied it to the phenomenon of evil.[272] Thweatt-Bates first established and explained chaos theory in a way that would be understandable to a novice to physics.[273]

Whereas Newtonian physics posits that precise knowledge of the initial state of a system combined with an understanding of the laws that

---

264. Wright, *Evil and the Justice of God*, 137–43.
265. Rausch, "Suffering History," 72.
266. Plantinga, *Breviary of Sin*.
267. Plantinga, *Breviary of Sin*, 14.
268. Plantinga, *Breviary of Sin*, 14.
269. Plantinga, *Breviary of Sin*, 67.
270. Plantinga, *Breviary of Sin*, 69.
271. Thweatt-Bates, "Chaos and the Problem of Evil."
272. Thweatt-Bates, "Chaos and the Problem of Evil," 60.
273. Thweatt-Bates, "Chaos and the Problem of Evil," 55–59.

govern that system would provide exact knowledge of all possible states at any given time, chaos theory posits that the initial state of any system cannot be fully known, nor can knowledge be precise enough to adequately understand the laws that govern the system.[274] The subsequent reality, according to chaos theory, is a temporary predictability of the system followed by an eventual unpredictability.

Thweatt-Bates then asked why does evil exist if there is a God and He is good?[275] Thweatt-Bates maintained "the qualities of connectedness and unpredictability in human interaction, suggested by its chaotic dynamic, are precisely those mechanisms by which evil is perpetrated and furthered."[276] Thweatt-Bates went on to describe evil as dynamic, progressive, and at its most basic level, a disruption of shalom.

Thweatt-Bates rejected a linear relationship between action and consequence, but asserted that the dynamic system of human life demands that evil has ripple effects that are not proportionate to the initial action. In tracing the blame of any specific evil, Thweatt-Bates stated, "Blame may indeed be assignable; but blame is ultimately corporate in nature, not individual, for we have all played a part in making the world the unsafe, unwholesome place it sometimes proves itself to be."[277]

Thweatt-Bates put forth a view on evil that is both Christian and harmonized with that posited by Boyd. Thweatt-Bates rejected the blueprint theology, and placed the responsibility of evil directly in the hands of humankind, as opposed to some divine plan.[278] Thweatt-Bates differed from Boyd in that there is no emphasis on the agency of spiritual beings, while mainly affirming the responsibility of human freedom. Additionally, Thweatt-Bates held a position opposite of Alcorn, and laid the responsibility of secondary evil at the hands of humanity instead of sometimes with God.[279]

Karmic Evil

This final section examines the ideas of beliefs about evil from a karmic perspective. As the notion of karma is most closely associated with the Buddhist school of thought, the only religion represented here is Buddhism.

274. Thweatt-Bates, "Chaos and the Problem of Evil," 59.
275. Thweatt-Bates, "Chaos and the Problem of Evil," 54.
276. Thweatt-Bates, "Chaos and the Problem of Evil," 64.
277. Thweatt-Bates, "Chaos and the Problem of Evil," 69.
278. Thweatt-Bates, "Chaos and the Problem of Evil," 68.
279. Thweatt-Bates, "Chaos and the Problem of Evil," 69.

Evil: A North Korean Christian Refugee Perspective

The sources in this section are the most esoteric in this research, as Buddhism teaches that evil is just an illusion and will disappear into nothingness. However, scholarly literature on Buddhism does provide some clear thoughts regarding evil, and can serve as an important framing point in looking at the beliefs surrounding evil on the Korean peninsula.

Contained in a text that looks at ethics from a variety of religious perspectives, Oxford researcher Morgan provided an organized and thoughtful explanation of Buddhist doctrine, especially pertaining to karma and the effects thereof.[280] At its most basic level, Buddhism teaches a principle of cause and effect: good things in this life are due to good actions an individual did in a previous life, and evil in this life is due to evil actions an individual did in a previous life.[281] Morgan examined specific Buddhist doctrines in regards to ethical questions, the explanations of which give insight to an orthodox Buddhist understanding of evil.[282] According to Morgan, the root of evil in the Buddhist worldview comes from greed, hatred, and ignorance.[283] These are not flaws inherent in human nature; rather, they are traits that obscure the enlightened mind from seeing clearly.

In fact, in Buddhism, there is no sin.[284] Karma is the universal principle that governs the universe; wrong acts create demerits which produce bad karma, whereas a good act or mental state creates merits which produce good karma. The good and bad karma that one produces affects their current life, and their future reincarnations as well.[285] Thus, if evil befalls someone, it is in some sense self-caused by their actions in a previous life. Karma is an inescapable force that is diametrically opposed to the idea of free will.

Moe offered a slightly different perspective on evil in the Buddhist perspective.[286] Writing as a Christian theologian from a Burmese background, Moe had a great grasp of both the Christian and Buddhist concepts of evil and suffering. Besides the foundational belief in God, one of the main differences between the Christian and Buddhist understandings of evil is teleological: in Christianity, good overcomes evil in

---

280. Morgan, "Buddhism."
281. Morgan, "Buddhism," 61.
282. Morgan, "Buddhism," 64–83.
283. Morgan, "Buddhism," 92–93.
284. Morgan, "Buddhism," 92.
285. Morgan, "Buddhism," 93.
286. Moe, "Sin and Evil."

the culmination of God's salvific plan, whereas in Buddhism good and evil both equal out and dissolve into nothingness.[287] This view of the inevitability of the destruction of both good and evil adds a considerable influence to one's perception of evil, as in the specific belief that evil is nothing more than a temporary illusion.[288]

Moe and Morgan both agreed that the karmic principle is the foundation of the Buddhist perspective of evil, and that evil, per Buddhist thought, is just an illusion. The emphasis on the teleological understanding of evil makes Moe's work stand out as different, which may be due to the fact that Moe does a comparative work as a Christian theologian.[289] Indeed, as was previously discussed, Wright emphasized a teleological understanding of evil in the Christian perspective as well.[290]

Buddhism as practiced in Korea may diverge from orthodox Buddhist teaching, so I must examine Korean Buddhist literature as well. A look into the Korean-Buddhist concept of hell and the afterlife by Lee offered an important insight on the topic of evil from an indigenous Korean Buddhist perspective.[291] By examining a *kasa*, a traditional Korean religious song/poem, Lee used a primary source to identify and explain how the Buddhist concepts of sin and karma were influenced by Confucian values of filial piety and proper family relations and obligations.[292] Men are awarded merits for being filial and for undertaking good works for society and country, while women are awarded merits for being subservient.[293] This source revealed how Confucianism is so prevalent in Korean culture that established religions such as Buddhism adopted its views of good and evil.[294]

Confucianism and Buddhism, while clearly having an interplay as noted by Min, have not always had positive inter-religious relationships, partially due to differing views of evil.[295] Muller dealt with the debate between Confucianist and Buddhist thought in Korea during the Joseon

---

287. Moe, "Sin and Evil," 40.
288. Kim, "Between Morality and Crime," 41.
289. Kim, "Between Morality and Crime," 40–41.
290. Wright, *Evil and the Justice of God*.
291. Lee, "Hell and other Karmic Consequences," 100–103.
292. Lee, "Hell and other Karmic Consequences," 102–4.
293. Lee, "Hell and other Karmic Consequences," 108–11.
294. Lee, "Hell and other Karmic Consequences," 101–2.
295. Min, *Korean Religions*, 3–5.

dynasty in the late fourteenth and early fifteenth centuries.[296] While this source could potentially also be categorized under the Confucian section in the literature, the content is more specifically on Confucian accusations against Buddhism and the Buddhist rebuttals. Using two primary sources, Muller detailed one of the preeminent assaults on Buddhism from a Korean Confucian master named Chong Tojon, and the subsequent rebuttal by the Korean Buddhist monk named Kihwa.[297] This debate illuminates differences and similarities in belief regarding evil that Confucian and Buddhist authorities held.

Both Confucians and Buddhists in the Joseon dynasty believed that the mind of humans was innately good, but somehow it encounters a problem that causes the mind to not manifest goodness properly.[298] This is an important point to establish, as Perrett highlighted the differences in the Confucian views of Mencius and Xunzi.[299] In the Korean context, according to the primary sources used by Muller, the Confucian view agreed with Mencius that humans are innately good.[300]

To the Confucian, the problem of evil was about social roles aligning with Heaven.[301] The Confucians accused the Buddhists of being selfish and evil by neglecting their filial and societal roles, and compounding their evil by teaching others to do likewise.[302] Chong Tojon also assaulted the notion of rebirth, and subsequently, the karmic tenet that actions in this life will have implications on a rebirth.[303]

Kihwa's rebuttals to Chong Tojon's argument synthesized the basic ideals of Confucianism and Buddhism, framing the Buddhist monk's abandonment of his filial and societal duties as an action which benefits all sentient beings, families included.[304] Kihwa reasserted that the karma principle is true in regards to good and evil; all fortunes one receives are due to previous good actions, while all misfortunes are due to previous

---

296. Muller, "Confucian-Buddhist Debate," 177–204.
297. Muller, "Confucian-Buddhist Debate," 179.
298. Muller, "Confucian-Buddhist Debate," 179.
299. See Perrett, "Evil and Human Nature."
300. Perrett, "Evil and Human Nature," 312–15.
301. Muller, "Confucian-Buddhist Debate," 180–81.
302. Muller, "Confucian-Buddhist Debate," 182.
303. Muller, "Confucian-Buddhist Debate," 186–87.
304. Muller, "Confucian-Buddhist Debate," 197–98.

evil acts.[305] Included in Kihwa's definition of evil acts would be ignorance, the killing of animals, stealing, and lying.[306] Filial piety as promoted by the Confucians is good, according to Kihwa, but not best. Filial piety can result in rebirth as a human. But only by rejecting love attachment can one escape the cycle of rebirth, a cycle that is not viewed in a positive light, but as a negative burden of existence.[307]

Muller's work presented primary source arguments for the beliefs surrounding evil of Buddhists and Confucians in Korea. The karma principle of cause and effect and a cyclical nature of good and evil was promoted by the Buddhists, while the Confucians explicitly rejected it. In his assertions, Muller agreed with Baker and Kim regarding the understanding that Confucianism views the universe in a delicate balance that is maintained by proper social order.[308]

However, Muller seemed to be somewhat at odds with Lee, or rather, their primary sources seemed to be at odds. The *kasa* examined by Lee used Confucian social roles to define what is good and evil from a Buddhist perspective, while the dialogue cited by Muller used the same Confucian social roles to accuse the Buddhist of evil.[309]

The examination of Korean Buddhism shows a lack of uniformity regarding what constitutes evil. However, there is a clear continuation of the understanding of karma that pervades Korean Buddhist thought. While the specifics of what acts are evil may be debated, the Buddhist perspective is clear regarding the nature of evil. Evil is self-determined by actions in previous lives, and ultimately is an illusion, just as the self is an illusion.[310]

The Korean religious understanding of evil can be categorized by grouping the beliefs regarding the agency and ontology of evil. The belief that the agents who cause evil are spirits is held by Korean shamanism, while Christianity, Confucianism, and *Juche* all teach that humans are the agents of evil. Korean Buddhism, meanwhile, posits that evil is an illusion, and bad events that happen are karmic in nature.

---

305. Muller, "Confucian-Buddhist Debate," 200.
306. Muller, "Confucian-Buddhist Debate," 195.
307. Muller, "Confucian-Buddhist Debate," 196.
308. See Baker, *Korean Spirituality*; Kim, "Between Morality and Crime."
309. Lee, "Hell and other Karmic Consequences," 100–111; Muller, "Confucian-Buddhist Debate," 177–204.
310. Morgan, "Buddhism," 92–93.

Evil: A North Korean Christian Refugee Perspective

In addition to the Korean religious understanding of evil, a number of studies have been conducted in order to understand participant perceptions of evil. In the following section, I will examine some of the prior studies on evil.

PRIOR STUDIES ON EVIL

Several empirical studies have been conducted that examine evil and suffering. In the past, studies have been conducted on views of evil and illuminated the impact of their understanding on the participants. The literature below is organized by the focus of the study of evil regarding responsibility, either human or spiritual.

Spiritual Responsibility

Several empirical studies have been done on evil from a religious perspective. One qualitative study conducted by two ministers and hospital chaplains, Bradshaw and Fitchett, found that participants all expressed a similar cause and effect belief about good and evil, namely, that good people and good behaviors are rewarded, and bad people experience tragedies and sufferings.[311]

Bradshaw and Fitchett used a narrative approach to understand how three different Christians have struggled with the question of theodicy.[312] While the three participants in the study all came from different Christian backgrounds, they all adhered to some sort of blueprint theology as described by Boyd: that God has a secret plan for every action, and is orchestrating all events.[313] Additionally, all the participants expressed a teleological hope beyond their current understanding of evil, as described by Wright.[314]

The cause-and-effect idea of good and evil that is described by Bradshaw and Fitchett is in direct contrast to the postulations put forth regarding evil and chaos theory by Thweatt-Bates.[315] This study opened a window into

---

311. Bradshaw and Fitchett, "God, Why?," 182.
312. Bradshaw and Fitchett, "God, Why?," 179.
313. Bradshaw and Fitchett, "God, Why?," 181–87.
314. Wright, *Evil and the Justice of God*.
315. Thweatt-Bates, "Chaos and the Problem of Evil."

the perspectives of lay Christians concerning evil, and offered an interesting connection point with the karmic understanding of evil.[316]

A quantitative study conducted by Daugherty et al. found that participants who came from more fundamentalist religious backgrounds had a stronger belief in divine determination surrounding evil.[317] Daugherty et al. used a psychological lens and developed and tested a new psychometric scale.[318] However, the instrument developed by Daugherty et al. was designed to measure to what degree participants believed God was in control of specific events; that is to say, to what degree participants adhered to a blueprint theology.[319] The participants were all college students who professed to be Christian.

This study and its constructed instrument were focused on the participants' perceptions regarding locus of control, internal or external. In other words, this study looked closely at what the participants believed about their own agency and the agency of God.[320] This study did not differentiate between human evil and natural evil, but conflated the two in the theodicy scale.

Another quantitative study conducted by Hale-Smith et al. found a clear distinction of the understanding of evil and suffering between participants with traditional theistic beliefs and participants with alternative belief systems.[321] In this study, Hale-Smith et al. developed an instrument entitled the Views of Suffering Scale (VOSS).[322] The VOSS evaluates a range of belief systems that are common in the United States, including theistic, atheist, Buddhist, Hindu, and unorthodox theistic perspectives.[323] The researchers sought to create an instrument that had a solid theological base and was developed through rigorous analysis, which the researchers contend was lacking in a similar study conducted by Daugherty et al., and was corrected in the VOSS.[324]

---

316. Bradshaw and Fitchett, "God, Why?," 182.
317. Daugherty et al., "Measuring Theodicy," 45.
318. Daugherty et al., "Measuring Theodicy," 44.
319. Daugherty et al., "Measuring Theodicy," 43–45.
320. Daugherty et al., "Measuring Theodicy," 43–44.
321. Hale-Smith et al., "Measuring Beliefs," 857.
322. Hale-Smith et al., "Measuring Beliefs," 855.
323. Hale-Smith et al., "Measuring Beliefs," 856.
324. Hale-Smith et al., "Measuring Beliefs," 863.

The study participants were all university students in the United States. The VOSS included nuanced views from Christianity, as the majority of Americans self-identify as Christian.[325] The Christian views of suffering represented in the study included what Hale-Smith et al. called the Free Will, Open Theism, and Word-Faith perspectives.[326] The Free Will perspective is associated with the Catholic and Reform Protestant or Calvinist understanding of suffering, while the Open Theism perspective is associated with the Arminian perspective on suffering, using Boyd as a representative example.[327] The Word-Faith perspective is synonymous with the Health and Wealth Gospel; if a person believes and prays hard enough, that person will not have to suffer.[328]

This study demonstrated that the beliefs surrounding suffering could be measured quantitatively. However, this study is significantly limited to university students in the United States, and is heavily geared towards Christian beliefs. The researchers concede that the VOSS is not useful outside of a North American context.[329]

A quantitative study conducted by Wilt et al. found that the beliefs that suffering is part of God's benevolent plan, as well as that a non-benevolent God causes suffering, were both associated with more divine struggle, lower levels of well-being, and higher distress.[330] Put another way, those participants that expressed a view akin to the blueprint theology described by Boyd had lower levels of well-being. This study utilized the VOSS instrument that was developed by Hale-Smith et al., and contained a sample made up of participants from several faiths, although Christianity represented more than 75 percent of the sample population.[331] As was the case with the study conducted by Hale-Smith et al., this study is limited to predominately Christian samples in the United States, and not generalizable for other cultural and religious contexts.[332]

---

325. Hale-Smith et al., "Measuring Beliefs," 856.
326. Hale-Smith et al., "Measuring Beliefs," 856.
327. Hale-Smith et al., "Measuring Beliefs," 856.
328. Hale-Smith et al., "Measuring Beliefs," 856.
329. Hale-Smith et al., "Measuring Beliefs," 863–64.
330. Wilt et al., "God's Role," 358–60.
331. Wilt et al., "God's Role," 354.
332. Wilt et al., "God's Role," 360–61.

Literature Review

Bradley et al. conducted a quantitative study to investigate what may influence the nonbelief in God amongst atheists and agnostics.[333] In the study, Bradley et al. found that, although the participants expressed intellectual reasons for nonbelief, negative relational experiences or negative conceptions of gods are seen as an important reason for nonbelief.[334] These negative experiences and conceptions include the idea that God is cruel and uncaring. In other words, the participants expressed nonbelief in God because they perceived God to be cruel and less loving.[335]

Building on the prior study of Bradley et al., Bradley et al. conducted a quantitative study and developed the Reasons of Atheists and Agnostics for Nonbelief in God's Existence Scale (RANGES).[336] This study found that

> Some atheists and agnostics experience religious doubt due to the presence of unnecessary suffering in the world (i.e., the problem of evil) . . . this finding raises the possibility that for some nonbelievers, the problem of suffering affects the desirability and perceived worthiness of god(s) as relational partners, and is not simply an intellectual challenge to the existence of a god or gods.[337]

In other words, some atheists and agnostics in this study chose to not associate themselves with a god because, paradoxically, they held god ultimately responsible for evil.

More recently, in a qualitative study conducted by Hall et al., which examined the discrepancies that Christian cancer patients experienced between their religious global meaning and their situational meaning, found that nearly two-thirds of the participants did not express experiencing tension, but rather experienced a deepening of faith characterized by expressions of God's love and control or God's personal involvement in the participants' stories.[338] The remaining third experienced theodicy questions, doubting God's love, justice, existence, or answering of prayer.[339]

The data of the study consisted of semi-structured interviews that were transcribed and analyzed using post hoc thematic analysis.[340] The

---

333. Bradley et al., "Relational Reasons," 319–20.
334. Bradley et al., "Relational Reasons," 325.
335. Bradley et al., "Relational Reasons," 325.
336. Bradley et al., "Reasons for Atheism," 263–65.
337. Bradley et al., "Reasons for Atheism," 272–73.
338. Hall et al., "Theodicy or Not?," 267.
339. Hall et al., "Theodicy or Not?," 269–70.
340. Hall et al., "Theodicy or Not?," 265.

participants in the study were all evangelical Christians in the United States who had been previously diagnosed with cancer. As this was a qualitative study, the product is full of rich data and description, and gave a voice to the participants.

The study furthermore suggested that Christians experiencing tensions surrounding theodicy should approach the tensions as relational ruptures in addition to cognitive doubts.[341] This study demonstrated that qualitative methods can be used to examine how a particular group understood their suffering based on their lived experiences, i.e. cancer, in light of the belief in a loving, omnipotent, and omniscient God.

In a recent article, Hall and Hill argued for the importance of including religious content in the meaning-making process in the midst of suffering.[342] Hall and Hill review the religious worldviews of Christianity, Buddhism, and atheism, and how the ontological, axiological, teleological, and praxiological assumptions in each worldview interplay with meaning-making.[343] This article demonstrated the importance of religious worldviews amid suffering, as well as highlighting the role that teleology plays in making meaning of evil and suffering.

Human Responsibility

An early phenomenological study to examine the experience of evil was conducted by Alford. Alford found that the participants in his study "defined evil in this way: not as a moral problem, not as a religious problem, not as an intellectual problem, but as an experience of dread almost beyond words."[344] The participants in Alford's study were a mix of incarcerated prisoners, university students, and working adults who came from a variety of faith backgrounds.[345] The participants were asked a specific list of questions in order to try and understand what evil meant to them, which were followed up with unstructured interview questions.[346]

Alford approached evil from a relativistic and existential perspective, using the discipline of psychology.[347] As such, the questionnaire

341. Hall et al., "Theodicy or Not?," 273.
342. Hall and Hill, "Meaning-Making," 470–71.
343. Hall and Hill, "Meaning-Making," 469–76.
344. Alford, *What Evil Means*, ix.
345. Alford, *What Evil Means*, 5–6.
346. Alford, *What Evil Means*, 156–57.
347. Alford, *What Evil Means*, 14–15.

focused on asking questions about the existence and nature of evil, with some specific questions on theodicy if a participant expressed a belief in God.[348] The questionnaire also contained hypothetical questions aimed at understanding if the participants found Nazi guards in concentration camps as evil; disturbingly, the participants generally identified with the Nazi guards instead of the Holocaust victims.[349]

Additionally, the participants in the study expressed evil as "that which threatens to obliterate the self, overcoming its boundaries."[350] However, Alford conceptualized evil as no-thing.

> Evil is nothing because it is no-thing. It is not an entity, not an experience, not a feeling, though it may be all of these and more. It is not a definition, even if we desperately want to make it one. We define evil because it scares us, because we do not know where it starts, or stops, so we try to confine it with a definition. . . . It is precisely the no-thing quality of evil that is so disturbing.[351]

Perhaps more than nothing, Alford frequently describes evil as a form a dread that is constantly trying to infiltrate people.[352] Natural evil and moral evil were regarded as separate, but the thrust of the study considered evil and humans.

While the contrast between incarcerated and free individuals was an interesting approach, the design of the study left some questions of credibility, particularly in the sample selection, the questionnaire format, and the analysis of the data. The participants in the study were self-selected (individuals who answered advertisements for the study), and the questionnaire contained several existential close-ended questions that could be considered as leading. The interviews were not recorded or transcribed, leaving Alford to take notes and then write reflections afterwards.[353]

Cerci and Colucci wrote a systematic review of prior studies conducted examining the relationship between forgiveness and PTSD symptoms in the context of human-made traumatic events.[354] They reviewed 13 previous quantitative studies, and found a relationship between

---

348. Alford, *What Evil Means*, 162.
349. Alford, *What Evil Means*, 17.
350. Alford, *What Evil Means*, 38.
351. Alford, *What Evil Means*, 117.
352. Alford, *What Evil Means*, 9.
353. Alford, *What Evil Means*, 154.
354. Cerci and Colucci, "Forgiveness in PTSD," 48.

forgiveness and lower PTSD-related symptoms in the participants. The studies reviewed by Cerci and Colucci were conducted in seven different countries, including South Korea.[355] Importantly, Cerci and Colucci postulated a distinction between forgiveness of collaborators versus forgiveness of principle perpetrators, where collaborators were understood to be less responsible for traumatic events than the principal perpetrator or individual who ordered the traumatic event to occur.[356]

A similar study to the one conducted by Hall et al. was conducted by Ahmadi et al.[357] In this qualitative study, Ahmadi et al. compared meaning making and coping strategies between cancer patients in Sweden and South Korea. The South Korean participants included Christians, Buddhists, and spiritualists.[358] The study found that the South Korean participants did not hold any spiritual force or higher power responsible for their cancer, but rather accepted the full responsibility for the cancer event due to high stress and over work.[359]

Ahmadi et al. interpreted this as the influence of Confucianism in Korea:

> Being responsible for one's own life and destiny is strongly emphasized in Confucianism, which may explain the mindset of the Korean participants, who have been culturally influenced by Confucianism throughout its long history (Pang, 1996). Korean participants often mentioned the Chinese character idioms . . . meaning "do your best, then God or High Power will do the rest."[360]

Most of the participants relied on healthy eating and prayer for healing, indicating a strong belief in both their own agency and the ability of God to heal. Like Hall et al.,[361] the participants expressed an increase in faith in God and spiritual powers by relying on prayer and experiencing increased health.[362]

Matos et al. also conducted a qualitative study that examined the meaning-making trajectories of Syrian refugees in the aftermath of their

355. Cerci and Colucci, "Forgiveness in PTSD," 50.
356. Cerci and Colucci, "Forgiveness in PTSD," 52.
357. Ahmadi et al., "Meaning-Making," 1794–811.
358. Ahmadi et al., "Meaning-Making," 1798.
359. Ahmadi et al., "Meaning-Making," 1799.
360. Ahmadi et al., "Meaning-Making," 1807.
361. Hall et al., "Theodicy or Not?," 267–69.
362. Ahmadi et al., "Meaning-Making," 1805.

Literature Review

collective trauma.³⁶³ Matos et al. conducted interviews and focus groups with Syrian refugees in Portugal to understand the reappraisals of post traumatic events and global meaning systems in the participants.³⁶⁴ The study found that participants had pre-war meaning systems and appraisals of the war, followed by reappraisals of shattered meanings and changes in psychological functioning.³⁶⁵ Importantly, Matos et al. found that religious themes were not salient in their findings, which surprised the researchers when considering the avowed religious identity of the participants.³⁶⁶

SUMMARY

Scholars have written extensively about the North Korean refugee experience discussed in terms of *Juche*,³⁶⁷ defection,³⁶⁸ adjustment to South Korea,³⁶⁹ and trauma.³⁷⁰ Additionally, there is much known about the religious understanding of evil,³⁷¹ along with non-religious understandings and descriptions of evil.³⁷² However, as some North Korean refugees have embraced Christianity,³⁷³ little is known as to how these individuals understand and describe evil. Thus, at the intersection of these bodies of literature remains a gap about how North Korean Christian refugees understand and describe evil based on their lived experiences.

---

363. Matos et al., "Syrian Refugees."

364. Matos et al., "Syrian Refugees," 3.

365. Matos et al., "Syrian Refugees," 5–6.

366. Matos et al., "Syrian Refugees," 14.

367. Belke, *Juche*; Cho, "Encounter"; Kim et al., "Reflections"; Ulferts and Howard, "North Korean Human Rights."

368. See Chun, "Representation and Self-Presentation"; Emery et al., "After the Escape"; Kim et al., "Pre-migration Trauma"; Lee, "Educational Experiences."

369. Kim and Atteraya, "North Korean Refugees' Intention," 1188; Poorman, "North Korean Defectors"; Yeom and Ward, "Integrating North Korean Refugee," 29–39.

370. Han et al., "Depression in North Korean Refugees," 283–89; Wolman, "South Korea's Response."

371. See Bradley et al., "Relation Reasons"; Bradley et al., "Reasons for Atheism"; Bradshaw and Fitchett, "God, Why?"; Daugherty et al., "Measuring Theodicy"; Hall et al., "Theodicy or Not?"; Hale-Smith et al., "Measuring Beliefs"; Wilt et al., "God's Role."

372. See Ahmadi et al., "Meaning-Making"; Alford, *What Evil Means*; Cerci and Colucci, "Forgiveness in PTSD"; Matos, "Syrian Refugees."

373. Jun et al., "Understanding the Acceptance," 445.

3

Research Methods and Procedures

THE PURPOSE OF THIS study was to understand how North Korean Christian refugees describe evil based on their lived experiences. In this chapter, I will provide the research methods and procedures used in this qualitative study. First, I discuss the design of the study and explain the philosophical orientation that I used. Second, I explain the data collection strategies that were employed in this study. Third, I discuss the method of analysis that I used to organize and understand the data that was collected. Fourth, I explain the strategies that I employed to ensure the trustworthiness of my research. Finally, I discuss ethical considerations that were considered for this study.

DESIGN OF STUDY

Qualitative research is an inductive process as "researchers gather data to build concepts, hypotheses, or theories rather than deductively testing hypotheses as in a positivist research."[1] The research conducted in a qualitative study produces "richly descriptive" data.[2] Additionally, the data gathered in qualitative research is often in the forms of quotes, interviews, and observations, and helps researchers to paint a picture of what they have learned about a phenomenon.[3] The researcher is the instrument and conducts the research with the participants to understand how the

---

1. Merriam and Tisdell, *Qualitative Research*, 17.
2. Merriam and Tisdell, *Qualitative Research*, 17.
3. Merriam and Tisdell, *Qualitative Research*, 18.

participants interpret their experiences and what meaning they might attribute to their experiences.[4] As this study focused on understanding the perceptions of the participants, qualitative research was the appropriate approach for this study.

Of the number of different types of qualitative research that can be conducted I chose to conduct a basic descriptive study for this qualitative research. According to Merriam and Tisdell, "All qualitative research is interested in how people make sense of their lives and their worlds. The primary goal of a basic qualitative study is to uncover and interpret these meanings."[5] As my stated objective was to understand the perceptions of the participants, a basic qualitative research study was the best qualitative research study design for my research question.

Philosophical Orientation

The philosophical orientation of the researcher has a direct effect on the research.[6] Butler-Kisber argued that qualitative researchers should explicitly state their philosophical perspectives in their research, and offered four main perspectives that qualitative researchers generally adhere to: critical realist, pragmatist, constructivist, and relativist.[7] My own philosophical perspective aligns with the constructivist view.

As such, I used a constructivist research orientation in this study. The purpose of the constructivist approach is to understand, describe, and interpret a phenomenon.[8] Because my research was aimed at understanding the how the participants understand evil based on their lived experiences, the constructivist approach was the appropriate choice for my study.

Merriam and Tisdell explained:

> Interpretive research, which is the most common type of qualitative research, assumes that reality is socially constructed; that is, there is no single, observable reality. Rather, there are multiple realities, or interpretations, of a single event. Researchers do not 'find' knowledge; they construct it.[9]

---

4. Merriam and Tisdell, *Qualitative Research*, 16.
5. Merriam and Tisdell, *Qualitative Research*, 25.
6. Starcher, "Qualitative Research," 55.
7. Butler-Kisber, *Qualitative Inquiry*, 5–8.
8. Merriam and Tisdell, *Qualitative Research*, 11–13.
9. Merriam and Tisdell, *Qualitative Research*, 9.

Epistemologically, I believe that reality can never be fully grasped, but is always seen through the lenses and biases. This means that what I and the participants perceive as reality is subjective in nature and socially constructed.[10] However, those perceptions of reality can be observed, recorded, and analyzed. As "qualitative inquiry is a journey of constructing meaning with people who share their stories with us,"[11] the participants and I co-constructed meaning and understanding of the data gathered through the interview process.

DATA COLLECTION

In this section I will explain how I collected the data in this qualitative study. However, in qualitative research, the data collection and analysis processes are "considered to be taken simultaneously and iteratively."[12] Thus, the steps I took were not done in a linear way, but rather as a back and forth between data gathering and analysis.

Selection of Participants

For this study I used purposeful sampling to choose the initial participants.[13] Purposeful sampling is a participant selection strategy "that will intentionally sample a group of people that can best inform the researcher about the research problem under examination."[14] For this study, I reached out to networks of North Korean Christians in South Korea that I am in contact with to begin selecting participants. Specifically, I contacted six organizations that work with North Korean Christians in South Korea. These organizations include churches with North Korean outreaches and non-profit organizations that assist North Korean refugees in South Korea.

Of those six organizations, four were able to connect me with individuals that became participants in my research, with every participant identified by the organizations as a North Korean refugee. After interviewing any participant, I asked for referrals for future participants, to utilize snowball or chain sampling.

---

10. Merriam and Tisdell, *Qualitative Research*, 9.
11. Starcher et al., "Rigorous Missiological Research," 51.
12. Creswell and Poth, *Qualitative Inquiry*, 84.
13. Creswell and Poth, *Qualitative Inquiry*, 148.
14. Creswell and Poth, *Qualitative Inquiry*, 148.

Research Methods and Procedures

Snowball, chain, or network sampling is perhaps the most common form of purposeful sampling. This strategy involves locating a few key participants who easily meet the criteria you have established for participation in the study. As you interview these early key participants, you ask each one to refer you to other participants.[15]

The participants for this study were Christian males and females over the age of twenty. The participants were all North Korean natives who have resided in South Korea for at least one year. The purpose for these criteria was to allow for the arrival and adjustment process that all North Korean refugees must undergo.[16] I provide profiles for each participant and organization in chapter 4.

Snowball sampling was appropriate for this study as the potential pool of participants is rather small. Furthermore, due to the sensitive nature of being of a North Korean refugee in South Korea, I needed to choose potential participants carefully and with recommendations or referrals from other participants, making snowball sampling the most appropriate for my qualitative research project.

Table 1: Participant Biographical Information

Participant	Sex	Interview Language	Translator	Connection	Age Range
Candice	Female	Korean	Miracle	Miracle	25–30
Chloe	Female	Korean	Miracle	The Café	20–25
Emily	Female	Korean	Personnel from The Academy	The Academy	25–30
Eve	Female	Korean	Miracle	The Academy	25–30
Faith	Female	English		The Maple Tree Inn	25–30

15. Merriam and Tisdell, *Qualitative Research*, 98.
16. Poorman, "North Korean Defectors," 103.

Evil: A North Korean Christian Refugee Perspective

Participant	Sex	Interview Language	Translator	Connection	Age Range
Gideon	Male	English		The Maple Tree Inn	30–35
Innocence	Female	Korean	Personnel from The Maple Tree Inn	The Maple Tree Inn	25–30
Jane	Female	English		The Academy	25–30
Job	Male	Korean	Miracle	Miracle	25–30
Miracle	Female	English		The Maple Tree Inn	25–30
Paul	Male	Korean	Miracle	The Maple Tree Inn	25–30
Ruth	Female	Korean	Miracle	The Farm	25–30

Interviews

In this basic descriptive qualitative study, the data collection consisted of intensive interviews, with the goal of obtaining, what Charmaz calls "rich data":

> Gathering rich data will give you solid material for building a significant analysis. Rich data are detailed, focused and full. They reveal the participants' views, feelings, intentions, and actions, as well as the contexts and structures of their lives. Obtaining rich data means seeking "thick" description.[17]

Intensive face-to-face interviews provided me with rich data that is thick in its description, which enabled me to build a solid analysis of the data.

---

17. Charmaz, *Constructing Grounded Theory* (2006), 14.

Research Methods and Procedures

In all, I conducted semi-structured interviews with thirteen participants. However, one potential participant was unwilling to give written consent and was therefore not included in the study. The final data was compiled from the remaining twelve interviews. A basic descriptive study does not have a required number of interviews. When the interviews were not producing any new themes or data, I knew that I had reached saturation, which "occurs when continued data collection produces no new information or insights into the phenomenon,"[18] and thus concluded the interview process.[19]

Length and Location of Interviews

The interviews that I conducted were in a range between one-to-two hours each. Due to the COVID-19 pandemic and social distancing rules, eleven of the twelve interviews were conducted via a video conferencing program, such as Zoom. Previous qualitative studies have effectively utilized distance interviews for data gathering, with several studies suggesting that participants may be more open to sharing in a distance interview than in a face-to-face interview.[20]

I conducted the in-person interviews in a discreet and private location to ensure the safety and confidentiality of the participant. This provided a space in which the participant felt comfortable to share details.

Language and Translation of Interviews

The participants in this study were given the choice to either use English or Korean during the interviews. If the participant chose to speak in Korean, then I was accompanied with an interpreter to have a fuller, richer conversation, as I am not fluent in Korean. The first participant in my study was rather fluent in English, and volunteered to serve as an interpreter for later interviews. I found this to be effective as she was a North Korean refugee as well, and so there was an immediate rapport between the participants and the interpreter. However, two participants in this study requested their own chosen interpreters for their own comfort. In all, three different interpreters joined this study. The interviews were transcribed and coded in English.

---

18. Merriam and Tisdell, *Qualitative Research*, 199.
19. Creswell and Poth, *Qualitative Inquiry*, 203.
20. Dzubinski, "Distance Interviews in Qualitative Research," 62–64.

If the interview was conducted with an interpreter, I transcribed and coded the English translations of the interview.

Regarding data collection in multiple languages, Marshall and Rossman highlight the use of interpreters in qualitative research:

> to lift the burden of absolute accuracy from transcriptions and translations. Our position is that this goal is a chimera; what we should aim for is a reasonable approximation of the interview partner's words and intent. Subtle nuances in meaning are signaled by punctuation and paragraphing (as in transcribing) and phrases and concepts generated in one language rarely translate directly into another.[21]

As such, the goal of the interpretation was for a reasonable approximation of the participants' words and intent. An area that I needed to keep in mind when it came to transcription is that people do not speak in grammatically correct sentences and neat paragraphs. As a researcher, I remained transparent and consistent about my own decisions as to 'clean up' or leave raw the verbatims of participants.[22]

I recorded the interviews using my password protected computer and later transcribed the audio file. I then reviewed each transcription while simultaneously listening to the audio to ensure that the transcriptions were accurate. Additionally, I checked the transcription for any identifying or revealing participant data and deleted it to ensure the security and confidentiality of the participants.

METHOD OF ANALYSIS

I analyzed the interview transcriptions via the coding process and utilized the NVivo program. In this section I will describe how I analyzed my data.

Initial Coding

I initially coded using a line-by-line analysis.[23] Line-by-line coding is especially useful when the data source is interviews, which was the only source of data for my study. The goal of this initial coding was to stick closely to the data in order to "gain a close look at what the participants

---

21. Marshall and Rossman, *Designing Qualitative Research*, 165.
22. Marshall and Rossman, *Designing Qualitative Research*, 165.
23. Charmaz, *Constructing Grounded Theory* (2006), 50.

say, and likely, struggle with."[24] Line-by-line coding helped me refocus later interviews, as this type of coding helped me "to identify implicit concerns as well as explicit statements."[25]

Focused Coding

During the process of line-by-line coding I also used focused coding to make the data coherent. Coding is an inductive process that moves from descriptive codes to conceptual codes.[26] The codes that I used in focused coding were "more directed, selected, and conceptual than word-by-word coding."[27] The focused coding helped to synthesize the data and allowed me to compare the participants' responses.[28] I did this by organizing the codes into categories in order to condense the codes so that I could understand any themes that emerged.

Memo Writing

Memos are "short phrases, idea, or key concepts that occur to the reader."[29] Writing memos during the coding process helped keep me "involved in the analysis and helps you to increase the level of abstraction of your ideas."[30] Another benefit of memoing in my study was that "memos catch your thoughts, capture the comparisons, and connections you make and crystallize questions and directions for you to pursue" and expedited the analytical work.[31]

While there is no set way to write memos in qualitative research, I wrote reflective memos after each transcription session and during each analytical session, as recommended by Creswell and Poth.[32] I used these memos to record the development of codes and themes that I saw emerging, in order to track the development of ideas in the research process. I

---

24. Charmaz, *Constructing Grounded Theory* (2006), 50.
25. Charmaz, *Constructing Grounded Theory* (2006), 50.
26. Butler-Kisber, *Qualitative Inquiry*, 31.
27. Charmaz, *Constructing Grounded Theory* (2006), 57.
28. Charmaz, *Constructing Grounded Theory* (2006), 57–58.
29. Creswell and Poth, *Qualitative Inquiry*, 188.
30. Charmaz, *Constructing Grounded Theory* (2006), 72.
31. Charmaz, *Constructing Grounded Theory* (2006), 72.
32. Creswell and Poth, *Qualitative Inquiry*, 188.

typed these memos on my computer and kept them organized in a file on NVivo to enable easy memo sorting and retrieval.[33]

Constant Comparative Inquiry

Instrumental to any qualitative study, including a basic descriptive one, is the analytical tool of constant comparative inquiry.[34] Constant comparative inquiry as defined by Butler-Kisber is

> a thematic form of qualitative work that uses categorizing, or the comparing and contrasting of units and categories of field texts, to produce conceptual understandings of experiences and/or phenomena that are ultimately constructed into larger themes.[35]

Through employing constant comparative inquiry, I organized the units of field texts into categories that allowed me to make comparisons across different individual experiences, events, and perceptions of phenomena.[36]

There is not a single prescribed method to conduct constant comparative inquiry, but rather it consists of the process of organizing the data and making connections between them.[37] This is an iterative process that takes place throughout the research.

TRUSTWORTHINESS

In qualitative research, there are a number of strategies used to ensure the study is trustworthy.[38] The criteria that Merriam and Tisdell list to judge the trustworthiness of a qualitative study are credibility, reliability, and transferability.[39] Credibility asks if a research design is studying what it claims to be studying.[40] Reliability refers to if the results are consistent with the data that is collected.[41] As qualitative research does not claim to be generaliz-

---

33. Creswell and Poth, *Qualitative Inquiry*, 189.
34. Butler-Kisber, *Qualitative Inquiry*, 26.
35. Butler-Kisber, *Qualitative Inquiry*, 47.
36. Butler-Kisber, *Qualitative Inquiry*, 47.
37. Butler-Kisber, *Qualitative Inquiry*, 30.
38. Merriam and Tisdell, *Qualitative Research*, 242.
39. Merriam and Tisdell, *Qualitative Research*, 265.
40. Merriam and Tisdell, *Qualitative Research*, 242.
41. Merriam and Tisdell, *Qualitative Research*, 251.

able, as in quantitative research, transferability refers to how the findings might be applied in another setting.[42]

Strategies to Establish Trustworthiness

There are several steps that Merriam and Tisdell identified that a researcher can take to increase the trustworthiness of the research as judged by the criteria of credibility, reliability, and transferability. These steps include peer review, thick description, discrepant data, audit trails, and addressing the researcher's positionality.[43] I utilized each of these strategies to ensure the trustworthiness of my research.

PEER REVIEW

Peer review is a strategy used to support the credibility and reliability of a study.[44] This strategy involves having knowledgeable peers to read and reflect on the study to consider if the findings are plausible or not. My research is part of my doctoral dissertation which has had a dissertation committee in place to read and offer feedback on the research and its findings. The dissertation committee serves as peer review tool to help establish the credibility and reliability of my research.

THICK DESCRIPTION

Thick and rich description refers to a "highly descriptive, detailed presentation of the setting and in particular, the findings of a study."[45] By employing the strategy of using thick and rich description, the researcher can enable transferability of a study.[46] By creating a thick and rich description of the study context, individuals in a different context can assess the similarities between their own context and the study. Thick and rich description can be presented in the form of direct quotes from participants interviews, field notes, and other documents.[47] I utilized this strategy by including direct quotes from the participants to allow their own words to express their perceptions.

42. Merriam and Tisdell, *Qualitative Research*, 253.
43. Merriam and Tisdell, *Qualitative Research*, 259.
44. Merriam and Tisdell, *Qualitative Research*, 249–50.
45. Merriam and Tisdell, *Qualitative Research*, 257.
46. Merriam and Tisdell, *Qualitative Research*, 256–57.
47. Merriam and Tisdell, *Qualitative Research*, 257.

Evil: A North Korean Christian Refugee Perspective

Discrepant Data

Seeking out data that might disconfirm or challenge the findings of research is a strategy that is called discrepant case analysis, or more simply, including discrepant data.[48] In my study, when themes emerged in the research, I would intentionally look for evidence that supports an alternative explanation.[49] I included any discrepant data in my findings in order to provide "a realistic assessment of the phenomenon under study."[50] This strategy helped to establish the credibility and transferability of the research, as the inability to find any alternative explanations increases the confidence in initial explanation.[51]

Audit Trail

Qualitative researchers can increase the credibility and reliability of a study by utilizing the strategy of audit trails.[52] Audit trails are used to "describe in detail how data were collected, how categories were derived, and how decisions were made throughout the inquiry."[53] I kept a detailed journal of my research process, which also included memoing as I coded and analyzed my data. I also sent regular reports to my dissertation chair that included a summary of what I had done, what problems I was experiencing, and what plans I was making for the next steps of the research process.

Researcher's Positionality

Positionality, or the researcher's position, refers to how the researcher affects and is affected by the research process.[54] Positionality is the researcher's own placement, social, locational, ideological, relative to the research project or to the participants in it.[55] By making my own perspectives, biases, and positions clear to the reader, the reader is enabled to better understand how my values and expectations may influence the

---

48. Merriam and Tisdell, *Qualitative Research*, 249.
49. Merriam and Tisdell, *Qualitative Research*, 249.
50. Creswell and Poth, *Qualitative Inquiry*, 261.
51. Merriam and Tisdell, *Qualitative Research*, 249.
52. Merriam and Tisdell, *Qualitative Research*, 252–53.
53. Merriam and Tisdell, *Qualitative Research*, 252.
54. Merriam and Tisdell, *Qualitative Research*, 249.
55. Glesne, *Becoming Qualitative Researchers*, 151.

Research Methods and Procedures

conduct and conclusions of the study.[56] A greater window into my own biases, thus, allows the reader to have increased trust in the credibility and reliability of the research findings.

I am a white, American, educated male, who has not suffered displacement, government oppression, or other significant traumatic events. The participants will all have come from one of the most repressive regimes in the world, escaped at the risk of their own lives, suffered traumas because of displacement and readjustment. Some female participants, in particular, have suffered gender-based violence in North Korea or during their journey to South Korea.[57] Furthermore, some participants have experienced a level of discrimination in South Korea as they are sometimes viewed as backwards with what can be perceived by South Koreans as strange and outdated traditions and habits they learned in North Korea.[58]

I approached this research aware of how my gender, experiences, ethnicity, and nationality may have impacted the participants. I worked to establish rapport with all the participants by affirming that I was interested in their story. I also refrained from making any political or judgmental statements. I also bracketed my own feelings of shock, sadness, or anger that I experienced during the interviews to not unduly influence the participants to respond differently. However, I did express empathy to the participants in order to encourage their continued sharing and to build rapport. I used reflective memoing after interviews and during the coding process to remain aware of and monitor my positionality.

ETHICAL CONSIDERATIONS

The trustworthiness of a study depends on the ethics of the investigator.[59] Qualitative researchers have compiled a variety of ethical issues that may arise during the research process, and a variety of approaches to address these ethical issues.[60] The Belmont Report, published in 1979 by the National Commission for the Protection of Human Subject of Biomedical and Behavioral Research, established three ethical principles in human-focused

---

56. Merriam and Tisdell, *Qualitative Research*, 249.
57. Emery et al., "After the Escape," 1001.
58. Chun, "Representation and Self-Presentation," 99.
59. Merriam and Tisdell, *Qualitative Research*, 260.
60. Creswell and Poth, *Qualitative Inquiry*, 53–58; Glesne, *Becoming Qualitative Researchers*, 158–80; Merriam and Tisdell, *Qualitative Research*, 260–65.

research: respect, beneficence, and justice.[61] I will use these three principles as the central framework for developing my ethical consideration.

The ethical standards for respecting participants involve obtaining voluntary and informed consent from the participants.[62] The beneficence principle places the ethical standard on the researcher to not cause emotional stress on the participants, and to protect the privacy of the participants.[63] The justice principle refers to the emphasis placed on sharing the benefits and the burdens of the research between the participants and the researcher.[64]

In order to ensure my research is conducted in an ethical manner I undertook a number of steps. First, I protected the identity of the participants by using pseudonyms in all oral and written reports and subsequent articles. No personal identifying statements regarding time, location, age, or type of profession were asked or revealed. Pseudonyms were used in the recorded interviews, as well as with all written documentation.

Almost all of the participants were all interviewed remotely, where I was in a secure location and the participants in a location of their choosing. The interview that was conducted face-to-face was the location of the participant's choosing. Participants were only asked to share to the extent to which they felt comfortable. The information gathered was recorded and stored on a password-protected computer, without any identifying features.

The participants were all told the nature of the study, the potential risks, the security measures taken, and then asked for a signed consent form. Some participants asked to give verbal consent, which I accepted in lieu of a signed consent form. Informed consent forms were scanned immediately after the interview and all paper forms were shredded. The scanned consent forms were saved in a password protected computer. All audio recordings were destroyed once the transcripts have been verified for accuracy and the research has been completed.

North Koreans refugees who are living in South Korea have arrived there by defecting from North Korea. North Korean refugees have knowingly and previously assumed risks to defect from the DPRK. The risks for defection include imprisonment and possibly execution for the defector or

---

61. Glesne, *Becoming Qualitative Researchers*, 159.
62. Glesne, *Becoming Qualitative Researchers*, 160.
63. Glesne, *Becoming Qualitative Researchers*, 161–62.
64. Glesne, *Becoming Qualitative Researchers*, 166–67.

the defector's family. As these risks have already been assumed, participation in interviews did not increase this risk level.

Due to the traumatic nature of defecting North Korea, it is possible that participants could have experienced pain from recalling their traumas. I was prepared for such an event with a plan to end the interview and refer the participant to a free Christian counseling center that is located in Seoul. However, no participant expressed a desire to end an interview at any point. I did ensure that one participant who shared about a specific sexual assault had access to a counselor if she desired counseling.

By taking these previously mentioned actions I established the research to be ethical with regards to respect for participants, beneficence, and justice. Additionally, I submitted my research proposal to the PHRRC for approval before I began to conduct my research.

SUMMARY OF RESEARCH METHODS AND PROCEDURES

In this research, I sought to understand how North Korean Christians describe evil based on their lived experiences. As this study was focused on the perceptions of the participants, I conducted a constructivist basic qualitative study.

I gathered data from participants who fit the criteria, using purposeful and snowball sampling methods. I conducted semi-structured interviews to gather the data. I transcribed the interviews and then analyzed the data by coding the transcriptions using NVivo software.

In order to ensure the trustworthiness of the study I utilized the following strategies: peer review, thick description, discrepant data, audit trails, and the researcher's position. Additionally, the research was conducted in an ethical manner that is consistent with the approval of the PHRRC.

4

Participants

IN THIS CHAPTER I will introduce each of the twelve participants of this study along with some of their respective stories. I selected my participants by contacting six organizations that work with North Korean Christians in South Korea. Of those six organizations, four were able to connect me with individuals who became participants in my research. To protect the identities of the participants and of the organizations, I will refer to them with pseudonyms.

First, I have compiled the participants into the table above. Included in the table is relevant biographical information and how I connected with each of them. Then I introduce each of the participants in alphabetical order. In each case I use some of their own words to tell their stories. The participant biographies capture aspects of each participants' story that are important in understanding the background and context of their lived experiences. Some participants have experienced hardships that include starvation, abandonment, human trafficking, and imprisonment. These hardships are part of the lived experiences from which they describe their understanding of evil.

CANDICE

Candice is a woman in her thirties. She fled North Korea as a teenager, and remained in hiding in China for about ten years. Candice became a Christian while staying with some Christian family members when she was living in China.

Her interview was quite interesting, as she had unique stories and was honest about her own failures and shortcomings. She was the only participant to discuss the murder of a family member at the hands of the North Korean government. Candice shared about the tough decisions she had to make while in China in order to avoid being sent back to North Korea. Candice admitted:

> During that time, I was not a member of the church, but I was a defector, but since I started living there for a long time the police suspected me. So, I was brought to the police. An officer interrogated me and figured out that I was a North Korean. And the officer asked me to inform him of the things, the work, that the pastor does for the defectors at the church. With the condition that "if you tell me everything about the pastor's work, I will protect you while living in China." So, I said "yes," and I was released from prison. So, I used to meet the officer two or three times in a week.

However, the church realized what was happening and sent Candice to South Korea for her protection and the protection of the church.

I was introduced to Candice through her friend, Miracle. As Candice is not yet fluent in English, Miracle joined the interview to interpret for us.

CHLOE

Chloe is under the age of twenty-five, and the youngest participant I interviewed. She is currently in university in South Korea, studying to be a nurse. Chloe explained that she left North Korea due to poverty and not having any future there. She stated, "We were so poor. Including me there are three siblings—one boy and two girls. After elementary school I couldn't go to middle school or high school due to the poorness of my family situation."

When Chloe was still a child, she had to surrender any dreams for her future and had to work to help provide for her family. Chloe shared:

> Even though I was so young I had to start working for a living. It is the time to have a dream and vision, you know, in middle school and high school. But I couldn't express my desire and dreams to my parents, because I understood the situation in my family. So, I have to give up all my dreams.

Chloe became depressed and decided to try and escape North Korea or die trying. After successfully escaping, she stayed in Laos with a missionary for three months. During that time, she became a Christian.

Evil: A North Korean Christian Refugee Perspective

My first meeting with Chloe was our interview, after becoming connected through The Café. Chloe was not confident in her English ability, so Miracle interpreted our interview.

EMILY

Emily is a woman in her mid-twenties who is a university student. Out of the study participants, Emily arrived in South Korea most recently. Her interview was unique in a number of ways. She had several very traumatic stories that she recounted in great detail; for example, she was the only participant to discuss personally experiencing sexual assault while escaping. Emily was also the only participant who had a family member get unknowingly trafficked. This was the only interview conducted face to face and not through video chat.

Emily escaped North Korea with her mother and sister because of poverty. Emily had this to say about her experience:

> Then we had almost no money. So, we put all our money together and entered the border line where North Korea and China meet. At the border line we spent one month trying to find a broker to get into South Korea. It was during that time my mom heard that if you cross over and just work for two months in China you'll have enough money that you can come back and live pretty well. So, my mom's plan and thinking was that we will cross over into China and work for two months and then we can cross back over and live well in North Korea.

However, instead of working for a short time and returning to North Korea, Emily and her sister were separated from their mother the day they arrived in China. They did not meet again until they were all in South Korea a decade later.

Emily lived in a Christian orphanage in China for several years with her sister. She then lived in a church leader's home in China, where she began to consider Christianity through the witness and kindness of her host family. After a few years, she became a Christian.

I met Emily through The Academy, who also sent a woman, Emily's mentor, to interpret for the interview, which may have helped Emily feel comfortable enough to go in depth in sharing her stories.

EVE

Eve is a woman in her late twenties. I became connected with Eve through The Academy. Eve is the only participant to recount hearing a bit about God and the story of Jesus while in North Korea with her family. Eve shared:

> My parents used to smuggle, so they had a relationship with China and could bring in some movies about God from China. And we watched several movies about Jesus. And watching the movies my parents came to believe about God, especially when they crossed the border from China, and into South Korea, pastors helped my parents make it to South Korea. So they started going to church as soon as they arrived in South Korea.

Through her parents' smuggling Eve was exposed to Christianity. She continued her story:

> When I was fourteen years old in North Korea I watched a South Korean movie in my house by my father's friend who gave me a USB. In the USB there were several movies, and I found there was one about God. And I could see people praying and believing in God for the first time.

That experience planted a seed of faith in Eve, and she began to pray throughout difficult experiences. About her escape experience, Eve said:

> When I was watching the movie, I didn't realize why people were dead and why Jesus died for people. I didn't understand all those stories. But when I was crossing the river between North Korea and China, I prayed a lot for helping, even though I didn't really know about God. But whenever I faced challenges in my life in North Korea, such as being under surveillance by the North Korean police after my parents left North Korea first, I always kept praying by myself. So, by this I came to know God.

She was the only participant who had lived in Pyeongyang, which was a symbol of status for her family. Because Eve was not confident in her English ability, Miracle helped interpret the interview.

FAITH

Faith is a woman in her early thirties, who has recently graduated university and is a teacher in South Korea. Faith had a unique escape experience, as for a period of time children without citizenship in China were able to obtain citizenship. Faith shared:

> Because I was so young when I went to China, so at that time, the Chinese government kind of decided those who don't have citizenship to have a chance to get it. Because a lot of Chinese kids were unable to have that citizenship as well, because there are so many population. So, they have this one child policy, but at that time they were allowing and including me to have it. So, I was lucky.

Faith spent several years in China, where she would convert to Christianity through attending church with her mother and step-grandmother. Faith shared about how she became a Christian:

> So, my step-grandmother, she was a Christian in China. So, she let my mom go to church, because I was so young I didn't have any choice, so I just followed my mom. And as I go to church it became kind of like a habit, but as time goes by I started to trust Jesus. Because every time I pray, I kind of notice a lot of my wishes come true. And even though it's not [wishes don't come true], later I will always understand that wasn't a good timing. So maybe it wasn't the best time to achieve that goal, but later on, I find out, "Oh, it's a better way." So, I could do something better. So, I just begin believing in Jesus, since I was young.

She later followed her mother to South Korea to claim asylum. She said this about that experience:

> So, then my mom came to Korea first, and then she made all the process to make me. She invited me for this travel tourist visa. And then, yes. So, I just, it was so easy. Maybe it was complex process for my mom, but for me it was easy.

Faith and I met at a meeting hosted by The Maple Tree Inn, where I also met Miracle. As she is fluent in English, my interview with Faith was conducted in English without a translator.

GIDEON

Gideon is a young man in his late twenties, who is currently completing his university studies in computer science. Gideon escaped with the help of his mother after graduating high school. After crossing the border into China, their broker never showed up, leaving them stranded. Gideon recounted:

> So, my mom and I were just in China without anyone's help. We didn't have any money, we didn't have anything to do. So, we wandered the streets about two days. And we didn't have any

food. My mom and I thought it really was the end of our lives. Because we can't find anyone who can help us. But suddenly my mom saw the cross. And she had heard some stories about church; if someone goes there, the church helps them.

The church helped house and feed Gideon and his mother for a season, until they were able to escape China for South Korea. Gideon remembered that time in his life:

> And I had lots of time in China, and the church was right in front of our house, so I went there every day almost. Because I didn't have anything to do; I didn't know anything about China. From that point I believed in God. And also, during the journey to South Korea, it's very dangerous. So, I always prayed to my God, "Help me please be safe." For us it was very important. It was related to our life and our future. But finally, he helped us to come to South Korea. That's why when I came to South Korea I prayed to God, "Thank you! Thanks! Thanks! Thanks!" Praying almost every day. And until now I am very thankful to my God to rescue us from North Korea.

Gideon converted to Christianity as a result of those Christians who helped him and his mother.

Gideon, whom I met through The Maple Tree Inn, was the first male I interviewed during the research. He was confident in English and so his interview was conducted in English.

INNOCENCE

Innocence is woman in her mid-twenties, and is currently studying nursing in university. Innocence initially escaped North Korea, looking for work in China. Innocence shared this about her experience:

> I needed money to go to college and to help my parents and my sister. And I just didn't think it would be a difficult thing; I thought it would be easy to go and make money and come back.

While in China, Innocence was abandoned by her broker and had to escape to South Korea. Innocence recounted converting to Christianity when she was in the Hanawon system in South Korea, saying:

> I got to know Jesus in a facility that protected North Koreans. At that time, I could choose a religion. So, I went to the Catholic a little while, however I went to Christian [Protestant] again, because my

> mind was still anxious and hard. I cried for one hour after hearing the praise song for the first time. I had a headache because I cried a lot, but my mind was very comfortable. And I was praying while calling Jesus' name. I started to get to know Jesus from then on.

I asked Innocence what stood out about the Protestant service to her, and she began discussing the Korean idea of *Han*.

> Innocence: There is a Korean way of expressing this. Before I selected Christianity, we had an opportunity to visit the three religions. I went to the Catholic Mass, and I went to the Confucianism, no not Confucianism but Buddhist worship or temple, and then I went to the Christian worship as well. When I went to the Catholic and the Buddhist temple I didn't feel what I felt when I attended the Christian worship. And what I felt at the Christian worship was, are you familiar with Han?
>
> Ryan: Yes, Han, suffering.
>
> Innocence: Yes, Han. I felt that when I went to the Christian worship that Han was like released.

I asked if she had another experience in which she felt that Han was released, and she said:

> I never had Han before; all the Han I experienced was my journey from North Korea to China and South Korea. So, I've never thought about that. The Han that I released was at the Christian worship was the hardship, the journey, to South Korea.

I met Innocence through The Maple Tree Inn. Her English is proficient, but she wanted an interpreter to help. She asked for a specific woman from The Maple Tree Inn, who had already heard Innocence's story and was fluent in English

JANE

Jane is a woman in her late twenties whom I met through The Academy. Jane is in university in South Korea, studying to be a lawyer. Her dream is to work as a human rights lawyer, based on her own experience of being imprisoned in North Korea. Jane told me that she wanted to be a lawyer "because I want to fight for what is true and just to help people because they don't have any human rights," so she began to study law.

Participants

While several participants experienced prison in China, Thailand, or Laos, Jane was the only participant who discussed being personally imprisoned in North Korea, and thus offers a unique perspective.

Jane became a Christian while staying with a group of missionaries after escaping North Korea. She shared this about her experience:

> So, at that time, I met some missionaries in Laos, and there I studied for three months about Jesus and the Bible. At the first I thought that Jesus was just a fraud. He was just smart and made up some stuff to try to fraud people, and Jesus just lied, he was a liar; I thought that. And then I became a Christian through some time and getting some experience.

She grew further in her faith after living with a church leader for a few years. Jane knows English, so I did not use a translator for the interview.

JOB

Job is a man in his late twenties who is currently working in South Korea. Job was one of the few participants who had experienced the famine in North Korea, and his stories reflected the difficulty of that period. Job was sent to China and then South Korea as a teenager by his family because he was starving without food in North Korea.

Job first encountered Christianity while he was in China. He recounted his story for me:

> First of all, I knew about Christianity in China when I was staying there. In China I saw the Christmas trees and the lights during the Christmas period. I asked my friends about that and they said it was for Jesus' birthday. But I didn't go to church or believe, and no one told me about Christianity honestly.

Job became a Christian while studying in university in South Korea. A church ministry gave North Korean students scholarships for school, so Job became involved in that church. Job recounted his experience:

> Then in my 20s, after I attended university, there was a junior who said that there is an organization that helps students study. He asked me if I would go and I said yes. So I followed him there and there I came to know about Christianity. So little by little I started going to church at the time. But even though I started going to church, I didn't believe in Jesus honestly. But my purpose was to study and to learn at the church. . . . I started going to [church]

79

when I was twenty-three years old because the church provides scholarships for North Korean students. So, I wasn't such a holy Christian, but for the money at first, I started going to church. Even though I didn't have a deep belief or faith towards God I attended the worship and the Sunday preacher every Sunday.

Job grew in his faith, and helped serve in missions activities abroad. I was introduced to Job through Miracle, who also helped interpret his interview.

MIRACLE

Miracle is a woman in her late twenties, currently studying at university in Seoul. Miracle escaped North Korea as a teenager. She crossed the Tumen River into China alone, jumped into the first taxi she saw, and asked for help to get to South Korea. Thankfully, the taxi driver did not turn Miracle into the police. Miracle recounted:

> And he brought me to a church because he didn't know any broker who could help me. But instead, he told me, "As long as you are honest whatever you say, then people in church can help you. So be honest."

At that church, Miracle was taken care of and began to join in the morning prayer services. Although she did not have any prior exposure to Christianity, she began to read the Bible and listen to the worship songs. She continued to share about her experience in China:

> So every morning I woke up so early and went to church and prayed. And tried reading the Bible. At the beginning I said that the pastor and all the people in church are insane, and that it's unbelievable. What is God? What is Jesus? Like that. I've never heard about that. I never heard in North Korea about that. So it was really new, and unreality in my view. But after a couple of days, I started to feel that all the words in the Bible are very educational and really warm and nice.

She became a Christian while in China, and the church later helped her on the journey to South Korea. She shared about her experience becoming a Christian:

> I focused on reading the Bible. A few days later, at the morning prayer, I cried a lot, by listening to the song. . . . I don't know why it made me cry, but I cried a lot. And I felt grateful to God who allowed me to come to China without any help. I didn't have any

broker, but I arrived in China without any danger, so it was really unbelievable.

Miracle felt grateful to God for helping her escape North Korea. She then said that she felt guilty for things she did while in North Korea:

> Yes, that was the first experience, feeling grateful. The second was feeling, like, guilty. I felt that. Even though I didn't know God in North Korea, but reading the Bible and listening to preaching, I came to recognize that I made lots of sins in North Korea. So I think both of them [the feelings made me cry] really.

I asked Miracle what she felt guilty for, and she said, "[things] like such as, bowing in front of people, like Kim Il Sung and Kim Jong Il, you know?"

Miracle was the very first interview that I conducted for this research. I became acquainted with Miracle through The Maple Tree Inn. As she was fluent in English and Korean, I conducted her interview in English. She also assisted in translating for several other participants who were more comfortable participating in Korean than English.

PAUL

Paul is a man in his thirties who is currently studying architecture in university in South Korea. Paul was first introduced to Christianity in Laos during his journey to South Korea, where a fellow North Korean refugee gave him a Bible. While in prison in Thailand, Paul began to read the Bible, which opened him up to going to church when he arrived in South Korea. Paul shared this about his journey to becoming a Christian:

> So, in a prison in Thailand I used to read the Bible, even though I didn't understand it. Finally, in South Korea a pastor introduced me to a church. So that was the starting. . . . For four years I went to the church on Sundays, even though I didn't understand well about Christianity. But I enjoyed the songs at church and the worship. So little by little I came to understand the Bible, and I became dedicated to going to church. And then I joined the choir at church. I was blessed by listening to the worship and songs at church. That's how I became a Christian.

After graduating high school, Paul decided to flee from North Korea to go to South Korea because he believed he had no future there. He shared:

> I was in a dilemma, because I recognized that in North Korea that if I work I can't make money. Another reason was that my mom

had been sick for a long time. I wanted to change the environment surrounding me. So, recognizing that there was no future for me and it was hard to change the environment around by myself, I talked with my friend whose mom already lived in South Korea. Then, we decided to leave North Korea together.

I met Paul through The Maple Tree Inn. Paul and Miracle knew each other, and Paul asked that Miracle help interpret for his interview.

RUTH

Ruth is a young woman in her early twenties. Currently a freshman in university, Ruth escaped North Korea relatively recently. She was able to escape with the help of a friend who had previously escaped. She shared:

> I knew my friend who was living in South Korea. So, I was able get in contact with her. And my friend from South Korea sent a broker to North Korea who helped me to come to South Korea. So, I didn't live in China, I just directly came to South Korea by my friend.

Ruth, like Chloe, was too poor to go to middle school or high school. She fled North Korea to have a better future free from poverty. Similar to Innocence, Ruth became a Christian while staying at the Hanawon center after being impressed with the warmth of the Christians there. She shared this about her conversion experience:

> When I first came to South Korea I knew about the Bible and God, but not deeply. I also had the idea that I shouldn't be following any religion. However, I found the society, the atmosphere in South Korea is so confused and messy, so I thought that I need to have an organization or a group so I can be a part or a member. So one day I came to a church, and there I saw members who are so warm and they impressed me and were so kind to me. And I decided that this group would be so nice for me, so I decided to go to church at that time because I was impressed by them.

I met Ruth through The Farm, and our first meeting was at our interview. As Ruth cannot speak English, Miracle interpreted for us.

SUMMARY

In this chapter I have presented each of the participants of this study, providing some context of who they are and some of the stories that they shared.

The participant introductions provide some help in understanding the background and context of the participants' lived experiences. Some participants have suffered from starvation, while others experienced hardships such as abandonment, human trafficking, and imprisonment. These events of suffering and hardship are part of the lived experiences from which the participants describe their understanding of evil. In the next chapter, I will present the findings of the research conducted with the participants.

5

Findings

THE PURPOSE OF THIS study was to understand how North Korean Christians describe evil based on their lived experiences. The research findings demonstrate that North Korean Christians described evil as the oppression of the vulnerable, expressed in terms of government actions, including no human rights, public executions, and poverty.

The sub-questions for this study include how participants understand and describe: the causes of evil, the fallenness of humankind in light of evil, the sovereignty of God in light of evil, and the goodness of God in light of evil. The findings demonstrate that the participants understand and describe the causes of evil primarily based on human actions. All participants used examples of human actions to describe evil. Furthermore, participants described the evil as the oppression of the vulnerable expressed through the fallenness of humankind as seen through human trafficking, sexual violations, and discrimination. Participants described the sovereignty of God in relation to God's plan and God's timing. Additionally, some participants expressed questions and doubts about God's plan, both in general and amid suffering. The findings also demonstrate that participants understand and describe God as a God who cares about North Koreans and is a just God.

I will begin this chapter by presenting the findings in which participants describe evil as the oppression of the vulnerable, expressed in terms of government actions as no human rights, public executions, and poverty. I will then present the findings regarding the sub-questions of the fallenness of humankind, the sovereignty of God, and the goodness of God.

EVIL IS THE OPPRESSION OF THE VULNERABLE

All twelve participants described evil primarily in terms of a power dynamic where evil was described as when those who had power oppressed or took advantage of vulnerable people. For my participants, the powerful actors included both people and institutions. The North Korean government oppressed its people, the Chinese government and human traffickers oppressed North Korean refugees, men sexually oppressed women, and North Korean refugees were discriminated against by South Koreans, the Chinese, and other North Korean refugees.

Evil in Government Actions

All the participants in this study described evil in terms of North Korean government actions. Participants spoke generally about North Korean government actions as evil, with some recurring specific examples of North Korean government restricting human rights, holding public executions, and national poverty which my participants attributed to government actions.

When discussing their feelings on the North Korean government in general, eight of the twelve participants used words like "hating" or "resenting" the government. Faith felt that this would be the obvious position for most North Koreans who have made the choice to escape, saying, "I feel like most of the North Koreans feel the same way. Because if we liked the government, why would we come to South Korea? We're all the same."

Job felt very strongly about his hatred for the government in general, and particularly for the Kim regime, stating:

> So, if I had the authority to kill Kim's family, I would hope to kill them. Even though I would go to hell because I killed them, I would do it. I hate them. The Kim regime are a cruel group.

I was surprised at the bluntness of Job's comment, but he was not the only participant to speak in that way. Gideon echoed the sentiments of Job by personalizing his feelings of hatred towards the regime as well. Gideon shared his feelings:

> Of course, I really hate the North Korean government. And I really hate Jong Eun Kim, and his father and his grandfather. I think they are one kind of devil. They cause North Korea to suffer very much. They have killed lots of lives in North Korea.

Evil: A North Korean Christian Refugee Perspective

In discussing the current leader of North Korea, whom Gideon described as a devil, Gideon further elaborated what he meant, saying, "And also, in North Korea, there is Jong Eun Kim and his father and his grandfather; they took God's position. That's why it's really typical devil. They pretend to be a god." Gideon's perspective was that the Kim regime was acting as God in North Korea, something he attributed to the work of the devil.

Candice also highlighted the Kim regime when discussing the sins of the North Korean government, along with the victimization of the North Korean populace at the hands of the regime, "But North Koreans are innocent. They are victims of Kim's family. Kim's family has caused and created lots of sins."

Candice's experience of evil in relation to the North Korean government was quite personal. Candice stayed with her sister and brother-in-law in China for a while after escaping North Korea, as her brother-in-law was a minister who helped North Koreans escape to China. However, he was assassinated by the North Korean government. Candice shared:

> My brother-in-law passed away. He was poisoned, got poison acupuncture by a North Korean spy. He was so holy, he helped North Koreans a lot in China. At that time, I felt resentment at the situation.

This event shook Candice's faith and made her question God, stating:

> Why did God just leave him dead by that spy, by that bad person? Even though he was so faithful towards his work as a missionary. At that time, I resented God, and it was the worst thing that happened in my life.

After I asked if she still had those same feelings towards God about her brother-in-law's assassination, Candice replied,

> My head and my heart feel differently. I know that the disciples, when Jesus was teaching them, the disciples were martyred by people. Through that kind of situation others who didn't know about God came to believe, came to know about God. So, my brother in law's situation of passing away is quite similar; I like to believe like that. But it hurts.

Ultimately, Candice did not remain in hatred towards her brother-in-law's murderers, but rather focused on her pride of her brother-in-law's work for North Koreans. Candice shared:

> I am the third person, so I do not hate the person who killed my brother-in-law, but I am just sad. I am sorry. Because I believe his death was a martyrdom. So, I am very proud of him.

In addition to the comments about the North Korean government, three participants explicitly stated that they wanted the North Korean government to be overthrown. Eve expressed her desire for the North Korean government to end in conjunction with holding the Kim regime responsible for the suffering in North Korea, stating, "Also, for the government, I want the government to end as soon as possible. And be broken. Because everything was caused by Kim's family."

Ruth also echoed the sentiment that the North Korean government should be overthrown. She stated:

> My opinion is that the government should be overthrown. The North Korean government is a dictatorship. So, it should be overthrown. If I ask God about the answer, I wish that God would help to break the country, the government.

When asked about what a good government would do, Ruth replied:

> My opinion on good government is that the government should provide people with a safe living place and food. Like the basic things necessary for living. And with a good education system, and jobs. But the North Korean government doesn't provide those things to the people.

Faith did not limit her thoughts on evil in governments to just the North Korean government, but included the Chinese government's action of sending North Korean refugees back to North Korea, stating:

> They're evil. I kind of understand that they have no choice. But they, oh I don't know, I think Chinese government is evil. They're an all-communist country. So, they're not really a democratic country. So, the government is sending a command; they're commanding people to send North Korean refugees back.

I asked Faith to explain more about how she thought the Chinese government was evil. Her response highlighted other examples of oppression by the powerful Chinese government over vulnerable populations. Faith explained:

> So, they don't listen to other people's thoughts. So, like sending North Koreans back to North Korea, that's an example. In China

Evil: A North Korean Christian Refugee Perspective

> there are so many different ethnic groups, and Chinese government is claiming that Taiwan is part of them, Hong Kong is part of them, and that Tibet is part of them. So, every time people are trying to say, "Oh I am independent country," the Chinese government is giving them pressure. Especially that, Tibet, and the Uighurs, those kind of re-education camps.

Faith then expounded upon her thoughts that all governments are evil, emphasizing the power dynamics of those in control and those oppressed, stating:

> I hate the Chinese government, but the Chinese government is not the only country that is evil. I would also say that the South Korean government is also evil because they are weak, and the wealthy people, those big families are controlling. I don't know, so every country is evil, it's not only China. So, Chinese are being evil in their own way, controlling all the people and not listening to other groups' thoughts. And the North Korean government is evil and the South Korean government is evil. I would just say the Chinese Government are more evil because they give those minority groups pressure, so the minority groups have less freedom.

Faith, whose mother was captured in China and sent back to North Korea, was unique among the participants in that she expressed that the Chinese government was more evil than the North Korean government. When I first asked Faith to discuss an event where something evil happened, the first example she shared was about when her mother was sent back to North Korea. She shared:

> My mom was not with us. Yes. So, at that time, I was so insecure, because even though I know I have a younger sister, I have my stepfather, but I wasn't secure enough. Because actually, for me, my mom [chokes up] is the only person I can trust.

At this point in the interview Faith began to cry. After a moment of wiping her tears, she continued, "Yes. So, when she was not with us. Yes. It was so miserable."

Faith said that she was about eight or nine years old when her mother was sent back to North Korea, and it was several months before her mother was able to escape again into China. I asked Faith why her mother was sent back to North Korea, and she shared:

> Although I'm sure I cannot say who did that, I'm sure somebody just told on her. Otherwise Chinese police would not deliberately

Findings

to send someone to North Korea unless there's someone telling the police. They didn't really want to, but if someone tells this, they have no choice but to, right?

She then said it was dangerous for her mother to escape again, "Because there on the border, there's always somebody there to see if anyone is escaping. But yes. She always has to take a risk to come back to China."

Candice also felt the threat of being sent back to North Korea when she was in China. Candice's family in China helped other North Koreans who were escaping. She recalled, "I was brought to my brother-in-law's house as he was a pastor. At that time, he used to work for defectors who would visit China. He would give them food and gave Bibles to them." Because Candice's family home was a known stopping point for North Koreans, she was at risk of being noticed. Candice remembered what steps they took to protect her:

> When I arrived at my uncle's house I had to stay only one month. It was a small village; everyone was able to be aware of me. So, my uncle cut my hair like a boy for camouflage and bought me expensive clothes to hide me from suspicious view.

Candice had to change her appearance to keep from being found out and sent back to North Korea. After one month, she was moved to a different location.

In addition to general descriptions of the North Korean government as evil, participants highlighted several specific examples of why they believed the North Korean government is evil: no human rights, no freedom, public executions, and poverty.

No Human Rights

In describing the evil of government actions, ten participants highlighted the lack of basic human rights in North Korea. Jane decided to try to escape from North Korea because there were no human rights. Jane shared this about her decision to escape:

> And when I was young I thought about human rights, because lots of people around me some days go to jail, just go to jail, and that was tough. So, I think it's a crazy country. My country is a crazy country.

Evil: A North Korean Christian Refugee Perspective

She admitted complaining to her parents that she was born in North Korea, saying:

> Sometimes I was complaining to my parents about that, like, "Oh, why were you born here? Why are you North Korean? Because I'm sad that I am your kid." So, I didn't want my kids to tell me something like that in the future.

Thinking of her potential future children and the lack of human rights in North Korea put the idea of escaping in Jane's mind. She shared:

> And I don't want to meet someone and maybe have kids when my thought is "I don't have a future." Because of that, because it's a crazy country, and I don't want to have any kids there. So, I wanted to change my life for my next generation.

When I asked Jane what she meant by human rights, she explained about thought crime and physical violence, stating:

> Human rights, here is my point. If I had a thought, I could go to jail. Is that thought right or true, or is that a lie? I could get punched. Lots of punches at any time. That's human rights. We lost our rights. If I say something true and I didn't do anything illegally, they could say, "No, you're lying," and they could punch me. You can lose your teeth from getting beaten.

Jane's example of human rights violations came from her own experience. Later in the interview, Jane shared this about her story of imprisonment in North Korea:

> At the first time I went to China and then got sent back to North Korea and went to jail. There I got some special experience, because every night I could hear somebody yelling at somebody. It was kind of a nightmare.

Jane would daily hear guards beating other prisoners accused of lying to them. One older couple was beaten because they answered a phone call from their children who had previously escaped North Korea. Jane recounted:

> Their children escaped from North Korea to get money, and then they wanted to call them because they missed their mom and their dad, and then they called them and the parents were taken to jail. Then they got beaten. Merciless punching.

Although Jane believes that the physical violence was bad, she does not think that the guards were bad people; they were simply doing their job:

> Yeah, I don't think that they are bad people, because they are really. . . . You know, if I was in the position of a prison guard, maybe I could be just gentle and nice, but I'm not quite sure, because that position just requires them to do this. So, I don't think they are bad people.

Jane actually laid the blame for the prison guards and their actions on the government in general and Kim Jong Eun in particular. Jane explained her thoughts:

> Because Kim Jong Eun wants to get anything that he wanted, and whatever he wants. So, I think it requires for us to follow him, right? So, it's kind of like the structure of the government, the chain of hierarchy. People don't, people can't escape from them. So, it makes them do things. Because nobody wants to be poor, nobody wants bad things. Just because normal people and common people they also are inside and tell themselves, "This is crazy, this is crazy, I don't want to do this, but I don't have a choice." So, I don't think they are bad people, because they have the same spirit as we do.

This prison experience helped Jane make the decision to attempt to escape North Korea again. She recounted, "Then I realized about human rights and what is important. And then I went back home and some of that experience made me think about life and human rights, so I decided again to escape from North Korea." After escaping North Korea, Jane is now studying to be a human rights lawyer.

Eve highlighted human rights violations as an evil of the North Korean government as well, specifically the lack of freedom of movement and expression, group punishment, and political prisons. Eve stated this about human rights in North Korea:

> Also, there is no freedom of movement and expression in North Korea. Have you heard about the worst prisons, for political crimes? Yes, if a family was discovered by the government doing something that the government says is criminal, all the family, to the third generation, will be punished by the government. Put in the political prison and executed.

She continued discussing the lack of freedom of movement by sharing her own experience of internal displacement at the hands of the government.

Evil: A North Korean Christian Refugee Perspective

Eve shared, "My feeling was that North Korea was not a place I could live anymore. And as my parents were expelled from Pyeongyang to [a different city]."

When I asked what could cause someone to be expelled from a city, Eve replied:

> My grandparents' social identity [caste] was not as good as others living in Pyeongyang. So, when the government decided to expel, to decrease the population in Pyeongyang, my parents belonged in that group. When I was a younger kid I was expelled with my parents.

Eve expressed the unfairness of a hierarchical system that would expel some groups of people from a city to the outskirts of the country, saying, "And I wasn't happy about that, and I wasn't happy with the hierarchical system in North Korea. Since I was young, I felt like things were unfair."

Gideon's story echoed Eve's thoughts on the North Korean policy regarding freedom of movement and political prisons. He explained why his mother brought him out of North Korea before he became an adult:

> If I'm an adult and I'm arrested on my way to South Korea I think I might die. I might go to the prison. Have you ever heard of "Soo Young Seo?" It's like a special prison. They put they people who want to go to South Korea or the political criminals, they put them in that prison. If people go there, almost 90 percent of the people die. It's a really terrible place.

Gideon clarified why it was better to escape as a child instead of as an adult, explaining:

> But if I'm not an adult they would give me some leniency because I don't have the ability to make the decision to go to South Korea. So only my mom would go there to prison, and then I might come out of a prison after two or three years. So that's why my mom wanted to take me before I became an adult.

Gideon then confirmed that his mother assumed the risk of being sent to an almost certain death in political prison herself in order to bring him out.

Chloe also mentioned the lack of freedom of movement as a reason that she considers the North Korean government evil. Chloe shared her feelings:

> I feel so sad about the situation. I can see lots of immigrants from South Korea that can go to other countries, but it's different for

North Koreans. Because South Koreans can visit their hometown whenever they want, and also, they are allowed to live in other countries. But for North Koreans, they have to move away, they have to escape. It's not allowed for them to visit their hometown. So, I feel the government is so evil because they make people in poverty but they treat defectors as traitors, and they may be killed by the government if arrested. So, I think the government is evil.

I asked Chloe if her thoughts on the government were personified by Kim Jong Eun, as some other participants expressed. Chloe replied that it was larger than the North Korean leader, but rather the entire government, saying, "The institution. Because it's too big to deal with the problem or the rules. Not only the individuals, not just Kim Jong Eun."

Job used the lack of human rights in North Korea to explain how the government is evil as well, saying, "There is no respect for humanity. Human rights, these kinds of things are not even allowed in that world. That place is really a hell." He later continued, "All these terrible situations are happening, such as political prison camps, public executions, and living without and protection of law and human rights violations." Job's thoughts and feelings on the North Korean government inspire his current work in supporting non-profit work in advocating on behalf of North Korean refugees. Job explained:

> We need to hurry and unify North and South Korea and fix these things. So, I thought, what can I do in [my city]? This why I participate in [non-profit group]. So, I feel like the North Korean government is the worst kind of evil.

Since escaping, Job has spoken in several different countries to advocate for the freedom of the North Korean people from the government.

Paul's thoughts on the North Korean government changed after leaving North Korea. While in North Korea, Paul was afraid of being punished for breaking any rules.

> If I was in North Korea still I would know what was wrong and what was right. Because when I was in North Korea I was scared of the society. And what the government said was wrong and right, and the rules that the government created, I believed everything what they said. So, watching foreign movies or media is a crime in North Korea. So, they punished people, and I agreed with the government rule; because it's wrong, people had to be punished.

Evil: A North Korean Christian Refugee Perspective

Paul continued his story, explaining his personal reasons for escaping North Korea, saying:

> My motive to leave North Korea was not because I disliked the government, or because I hated the government. But it was due to financial independence and I was hungry and was in poverty. So, then I made the decision to leave North Korea.

While Paul previously did not dislike the government, his thoughts have changed since escaping North Korea. When asked what Paul thinks about the North Korean government now, Paul stated, "I feel free. Currently I feel the government does everything wrong. Especially with human rights; there is no concept of human rights in North Korea. So, I feel anger and sometimes sadness."

Paul continued:

> Because they have a closed education system in North Korea. So, students are just allowed to learn from teachers what the government allows. There are limits on education. Plus, the public library in North Korea there are just several books, not a variety of books. So, it's hard to face broad knowledge. . . . I feel a little sad about the situation. The government limits independence of gathering information and knowledge. But the people have to take and people don't know about freedom. At that time, I didn't know that was wrong. Now I know and feel sad and sorry about the situation.

At the conclusion of our interview, Paul began to reflect on evil in North Korea, and whether it was due to government actions, saying:

> God loves us and provides us with free will. But in North Korea, they don't use the freewill. So, what is evil in North Korea? I wonder if it is the people that don't use their free will or the government?

Paul clarified that he was asking me that question. I told Paul I was interested in his opinion on that question. He simply responded, "I think it's the government."

Public Executions

Three of the three participants had personally witnessed public executions, and all three described them as evil. Two of the participants, Job and Miracle, described witnessing public executions as the worst evil they had ever experienced.

Findings

Job was a child when he witnessed his first public execution, and his recounting of the event was quite detailed and graphic. Job shared this about his experience:

> First, when I was about thirteen years old, at that time in our neighborhood there was execution of two women who were sex traffickers. Over the public speakers they were announcing that the execution was happening at a certain place and to come and watch. There were cars driving around making this announcement. We were young and didn't know much so were going to go to pick up empty gun cartridges and watch the execution. First, they tied up the women on a tree with a cross shape, put a white cloth over their heads, and then announcement why they were executing the women. Then from the right soldiers came out and shot like they were on a shooting rampage with their AK's [AK-47 rifle]. I say this. At the time . . . I still have dreams. . . . One woman got shot and it made her back bend forward. I could see bullet holes in her back and black blood was coming out. I didn't know human blood was so black. One woman unluckily got shot in her head and her brain fell out, a red thing dropped out.

As an adult, Job has come to understand that he suffered the effects of trauma from this specific event, and has categorized it and public executions in general as evil, saying:

> When I look back, I didn't really know, at the time that that was evil but . . . in South Korea, I realized this was the worst evil. How can you kill people in such a cruel way, especially in front of so many people as a public execution? I realized this was the savage North Korean way that has no respect for human rights.

Miracle also recounted a childhood experience of witnessing a public execution that she described as evil. She was clearly affected by the event, which came through in our interview.

Miracle shared:

> Yeah. I think the worst evil in my life was when I was eight or nine years old. In my elementary school I had to go to join the public execution. I didn't know even what is an execution when I was in elementary school, I was a kid, but the government forced us to watch a public execution. All the kids at the elementary school. And we had to stop studying. And we ended up going there. It happened in my hometown, not quite far away from my house. Soldiers shot four criminals. Because they sold drugs and

Evil: A North Korean Christian Refugee Perspective

> human girls to China. . . . It was the worst evil. And then it was the first time.

Miracle had to experience a public execution a second time when she was in middle school. After recounting those two events, Miracle began to express her strong feelings regarding the North Korean government.

> Miracle: Yeah, I still remember. So, I hate the government, and it made me feel disgusting.
>
> Ryan: On that story, and your response that you hate the government, when you think of something like North Korean public executions, what would you say you feel towards to government?
>
> Miracle: I feel the government, they are evil. And, they kill people. They kill people easily. And, they don't even, make a law about human rights. They are like, I feel they are like elites, they are not a government for public.

Miracle also expressed suffering ongoing trauma from her experience as an adult, saying, "When I came to South Korea, watching action movies, I used to feel like it was reality. I was really scared watching action movies or zombie movies even, like it looked true. It was a huge trauma."

Miracle, who translated for Job's interview, expressed that her experience of trauma in adulthood was due to witnessing public executions like Job.

Eve brought up the subject of public executions when she began to discuss the "evil things that the government does," saying, "I hate everything that the government does, but the worst thing is public executions and expelling families." I asked if she had experienced a public execution, and she replied, "I witnessed it once. I was young when I was forced to watch a public execution. But since I was young I don't remember the reason why the people were shot by the military." It was clear to me in this interview by her body language that Eve did not want to further discuss her personal experience of the public execution, but she did use the word "evil" to describe the event.

Poverty

In total, eight participants felt that the level of poverty and economic suffering in North Korea was the fault of the government. Out of those

Findings

eight participants, all expressed experiencing poverty as a reason they fled North Korea.

When discussing a bad event in her own life, Ruth's first example was the poverty that she and her family experienced. Remembering her experience of poverty, Ruth shared:

> In North Korea I couldn't graduate middle school and high school. Because of the economic situation in my family. . . . The reason why I couldn't go to middle school and high school was due to my family's economic problem, but I don't blame my parents, but I blame the government.

Ruth continued to explain her personal reasons for holding the government responsible for her family's poverty, saying "I feel it's the government's responsibility, because my dad worked for the government, but they didn't pay. It wasn't my parents' fault."

Later in the interview, Ruth explained to me why she felt North Korea was suffering from poverty. Ruth said:

> The North Korean government doesn't have any relationship with other countries. So, they can't have any export and import with other countries which is so important for their economic situation. On the other hand, the government spends a lot of money on the military. That's another reason why the country is poor, and people have to face famine.

In explaining the sins of the North Korean government, Ruth highlighted the government's responsibility for the poverty of the populace as the biggest sin, saying, "The period of famine from 1993. During that time more than two million North Korean people passed away. That was the government's biggest sin."

Ruth believed that the desire to escape North Korea because of poverty was common. When she discussed why she wanted to flee North Korea, Ruth explained:

> North Koreans extremely desire to escape North Korea and come to South Korea whenever they have the opportunity. So even though my family was not rich or upper class, I had my parents and my siblings. I tried my best to be rich in North Korea until I was in my mid-twenties. However, at that time I felt that there was no hope or future for me. So, thanks to my friend I caught the opportunity to come to South Korea.

Evil: A North Korean Christian Refugee Perspective

While Ruth is too young to have experienced the famine in North Korea, Job was old enough to have experienced the famine, and almost died due to starvation. Job said:

> My life was consumed with hunger when I was younger. The famine started in 1994, and I was an infant at that time. My family was poor, and we didn't have food. I couldn't eat my mom's breast milk. As we didn't have rice we ended up eating wormwood. But I couldn't eat it. . . . When I was ten years old, I had no food for four days. My aunt found me before dying; I was suffering from malnutrition. My aunt brought me to my grandmother's house, and for two months there I was able to gain weight.

Job expanded on his story of poverty in North Korea, starting from a young age:

> It makes me sad to talk about stories from North Korea. When I was three years old my parents divorced. And when I was five years old, my mom escaped North Korea. So I don't have any memories from when I was younger about my mom. When I was fourteen years old I spent a harsh time in North Korea, going to the mountains to gather wood. North Koreans need to go to the mountain to get wood and coal for heating homes. So, I had to go to the mountains to bring wood when I was fourteen years old, and I was so small. During that time, my mom lived in South Korea, and she connected with her family living in North Korea, and she asked about me. And they told her everything about my situation of suffering from malnutrition at the time.

After hearing that Job was suffering from malnutrition, his mother planned for him to escape North Korea and come to South Korea with her. He continued his story:

> So, she made her younger brother bring me to China. . . . So, I followed my aunt from North Korea to China, and in China I followed my uncle-in-law. And when I asked them, "Where is my mom?" They said that my mom was in South Korea, she was not in China. So, I called her when I was in China, and she told me that I had to go to South Korea to see her. At that time, I was [suffering from] malnutrition. It seemed like I would die from malnutrition. In China I had to gain weight to be able to escape all the borders. Then I followed a broker through China to Myanmar. And then I came to Thailand, and finally to Bukjawong and Hanawon.

Findings

Although Job's mother wanted to bring him to South Korea, Job remembers not wanting to leave China. He did not feel any attachment for his mother, and felt satisfied to finally be able eat enough food. He shared this about his feelings at the time:

> In China I didn't have any emotion towards my mom, but I was so happy that I wanted to live in China and not go to South Korea. So, I said that to my mom. My mom said that South Korea is much better than China so I should go to South Korea. But I didn't want to move and I didn't have any interest in my mom. She was just like an old lady, not like "my mom." And I was surprised to watch elevators and escalators in China, and looking at the huge airplanes. In North Korea, my dream was to eat the whole chicken alone. But in China I was so self-sufficient with the delicious meat and food and everything.

Job did eventually gain enough weight to be able to survive the journey to South Korea, where he rejoined his mom. When discussing a situation he described as evil, Job mentioned a tragic story of a baby who starved to death. He said:

> I saw a dead baby at the bank of a river. Someone had put it in a hemp sack and dogs had smelled it and gathered around it. It was a [illegitimate] newborn baby girl. She must have died while her mother was giving birth to her. So, I don't know, someone had thrown it away in the trash. I heard rumors about it from kids and followed to go see. I shouldn't have gone to see it because I struggled with that mental image even while still living in North Korea. When I saw it, I almost threw up on the spot. Later I heard from a man that he felt so sorry for the baby and buried in the ground when no one was looking.

When he was younger, Job viewed the situation of poverty as a tragic part of the reality of life. Job reflected about this experience:

> When I saw this, I thought of the rights of children and even now still, in North Korea if you're pregnant . . . how little did she have to eat that she ended up giving birth to an [illegitimate] baby and it died?

However, after leaving North Korea, Job said he now believes that level of poverty is not normal, but is due to the actions of the North Korean government against its people. Job explained his thoughts, saying:

Evil: A North Korean Christian Refugee Perspective

> At the time, I didn't know. Society was so harsh, North Korean society. I thought, "Of course something like that could happen." After coming to South Korea I realized this is not something that happens as a norm. It is part of the North Korean savage government's actions towards its people.

Candice, like Job, was sent by her family to China due to poverty. She shared this part of her story:

> It wasn't my decision to come to China. I was so young at the time, I was just a teenager, so I didn't know. My parents just decided to send me to China, because we were not rich and I have several siblings. So my parents hoped that me, as the youngest child, would have enough meals. But we didn't realize that we would never meet each other again.

I asked Candice if she has seen her family since she was a teenager, and she sadly said that she has not. I then asked her what her feelings were about being sent to China, and the thing that she shared was about having food to eat:

> I was happy at that time, because when I arrived at my uncle's house there were so many apples for me to eat. I really loved apples in North Korea, but they were unavailable there. But in my uncle's house I kept eating apples without having any other food.

At this point in the interview, Candice started laughing and said, "So, my uncle prevented me from eating any more apples." She then told me that she still loves to eat apples.

Candice's family suffered from poverty and decided to send her to China to have enough to eat, which ultimately left her separated from her family.

I asked Miracle her thoughts on the state of North Korea now, and she expressed that it is both the government's responsibility to care for the people, and that the government has failed that responsibility by prioritizing protecting the current regime. Miracle explained:

> Their responsibility is to care. To care for soldiers and the public. It's the government's responsibility, that they have to do that. But now the Kim regime's responsibilities are to make the public obey them, and to make them to become unthreatened, so they follow everything what they want. The current state of North Korea is the Kim regime's responsibility now.

Findings

Miracle also clarified that while she holds the Kim regime as ultimately responsible, the entire governmental structure and group of elites in North Korea all bear guilt as well.

Faith echoed Miracle's sentiments on the group of elites being responsible for the situation in North Korea. Faith shared her thoughts on poverty in North Korea:

> Groups of people who have the power already. So, it's not just one person, it's a group of people. People are all greedy and they all want more, and they don't want to lose anything they have already. So, in order to keep what they have they have to become a group and have to help each other to maintain what they have.

For Faith, the vulnerable people suffer from poverty due to the actions of those who already have power.

Emily's life was also significantly impacted by poverty in North Korea. When she was about seven years old, her parents divorced and both re-married new people. When her stepmother became pregnant, her father sent her and her sister away due to financial difficulties. Emily recounted her story:

> My dad put us on a train to go to our mom and told us to go live with our mom. So, I thought that my dad had already told my mom that we were coming on the train to her, but my mom had no idea that we were coming. To go from my dad's to my mom's we had to make one transfer on the train. But the ticket we had was only until the transfer; that was the only ticket we had. We had to get to [city]. We got off half way, and it wasn't continuing on. I began to ask the people around me if this was the train going to [city], and they told me no and that I needed to transfer on to another train. I said that "We don't have a ticket, what should we do?"

Emily and her sister were alone and stranded in a city they did not know. Thankfully, they were helped by the kindness of a stranger. Emily continued her story:

> That adult said, "I'm going to take your younger sister and hold her hand and tell them that this is my daughter, and that's how we will get on the train." Because if you are young, you can ride the train for free. So, the stranger took my sister and got on the train, and at the very last minute before it was pulling out I jumped on the train. Because I didn't have the ticket I had to get on after they were done checking the tickets. In North Korea, even though you

are on the train, they are going to keep checking tickets throughout the ride. For the remainder of the ride whenever the ticket master came to check the tickets I went and used the bathroom and the stranger kept saying that "this is my daughter."

Even though they were able to board the train, Emily and her sister were still struggling as they had no money or food with them. Emily remembered the generosity of the fellow passengers in light of the poverty in North Korea:

> The train went for two nights and three days, but we didn't have any food with us. For the ride the stranger shared her meal with my sister, and the other people on the train shared some food with us. Because its North Korea, doing that is not that easy because there is not much food around, so I understood that was not an easy thing.

Emily told me she was thankful for the kindness of the strangers on the train, and appreciated their sacrifice in helping her and her sister.

When they finally arrived at their destination, Emily's mother was not there to meet them. It was then that Emily realized her mother did not know that Emily's father had sent Emily and her sister to live with their mother. Emily continued the story of her journey:

> I realized that we were going to be orphans; that's what my thought was. . . . I was there with my sister and we went hungry for a whole day, because my mom didn't show up. My younger sister has a weaker consistency than me, so if she doesn't eat for a day she is weak and just has to lay down. Because my younger sister couldn't move I found a bench in the area and told my sister to stay on the bench. During then we waited for three days. For those few days we were just beggars.

Emily remembered that her mother used to sell things near the train station, so they waited until their mother might come. On the third day alone and begging, Emily and her sister found their mother. Emily remembers:

> I saw my mom walking by and I called out to her, but she didn't hear me. My thinking was that my mom checked in her stuff, so she is going to come back. So, we continued waiting and then around dinner time my mom showed up again. So, I said "Mom!" And my mom was very surprised too, and then we shared about the whole situation with her.

Findings

Emily's mother took them back to her home with her new husband.

However, poverty would continue to impact Emily's life. Emily's stepfather also had children of his own who lived with their mother. After Emily and her sister moved in, Emily's stepfather wanted to bring his own children to live with them. Similar to Emily's father and stepmother, Emily's mother and stepfather were unable to manage the large family, and ended up divorcing each other. Emily recalled how they survived after the divorce:

> So, my stepdad and my mom parted on not good terms. My mom was going to take me and my younger sister and just live together. The three of us moved back and forth between two cities selling things. We were selling the big traditional Korean jars or pots.

Emily, her sister, and her mother lived as traveling merchants. However, this lifestyle was impacted by poverty as well. One day, the jars they were selling were stolen, leaving them with no way to continue earning money.

Emily remembers:

> We would take those jars back and forth to try and sell them. We were afraid that they would get stolen, so we used to tie a rope around the jars and then tie it to us and sleep like that. Even though we had done that safe guard the jars were still stolen from us. They cut the ropes.

This theft is the event that precipitated Emily and her mother and sister deciding to flee North Korea.

Emily reflected on that event, saying, "When that happened, I thought that people are just evil and selfish and bad, just awful. Now when I think about it, I can understand the situation and the reason why they would do that." When I asked Emily the reason someone would do that, she understood it as needing to survive poverty, saying, "Because in the North the economy is really bad. And it's not like here in Korea when you work you are guaranteed to get paid. So, they had to make a living, so I understand that's why ... for survival." For Emily, needing to survive is an understandable reason the theft took place, but the root cause is the poverty and broken economic situation of North Korea.

Even though she holds the government responsible for the situation in North Korea, Emily believes in her own agency to affect change through prayer. Emily explained her beliefs:

> For me to keep saying that the North Korean government is bad or evil, actually my feeling is that is not going to change anything.

Evil: A North Korean Christian Refugee Perspective

> About a year ago I came to the realization to keep saying, "They're bad, they're bad, they're bad," is really pointless. I can pray that their thinking and their motives can change, so I began to pray that way.

Emily believes that her prayers can impact government leaders, who may then change their actions for the better. She said:

> Whether those government leaders believe in God or not, I can do something. I can pray that their hearts and then their motives and their actions can change. And that it can affect change by praying for their heart and motive.

Emily has transitioned from talking about the evil of the government to praying for the leaders to change.

EVIL AND THE FALLENNESS OF HUMANKIND

In this section I will share findings of how participants describe the fallenness of humankind in light of evil. While all the participants mentioned people in relation to evil, seven participants described evil as human trafficking, five participants described evil as sexual violations, and six participants described evil as discrimination. Additionally, some participants described evil as spiritual oppression. In each of these sections the participants describe evil as what humans do to each other, displayed in a power dynamic where those in power oppress the vulnerable.

Evil of Human Trafficking

While there is overlap between human trafficking and sexual violations, the data are presented in separate sections. First, I will share the findings in relation to human trafficking in general, and in the following section I will share the findings in relation to sexual violations.

During the interview process, seven out of the twelve participants discussed human trafficking as evil. Human trafficking was the term most participants used, although some participants used words like "sold" and "slavery" interchangeably with "human trafficking."

Chloe had the most direct encounter with human trafficking, as she decided to give herself to a broker to be sold in order to escape North Korea. Chloe shared this about her experience:

> I was working at the restaurant. At that time my best friend was at the same restaurant working with me. And a human trafficker,

a person who sells North Korean girls to China, introduced my friend to a broker. The broker said, "If you want to go to China I can send you there." Because my friend's mother was in a prison, so her family was poor too. It's really very easy for the brokers to sell to China because it's a convenient situation for them. So, my friend and I used to say, "It's much better for us to leave North Korea and go to China." So, we left North Korea with that broker.

Chloe explained that she had been depressed and wanted to die, which is what led her to decide to allow herself to be trafficked. Chloe shared:

> When I was eighteen years old, I was shy in front of my friends. I did not feel confident because we were poor in North Korea. I was working at a restaurant, and I secretly started to think, "It's better to die than to keep living." And that made me depressed. I was the second child of the three siblings, and when I was imagining about my marriage, the economic situation is the standard in North Korea to get married with a nice guy, and it made me even sadder. Finally, I decided to go to China because I recognized that if I die by myself in North Korea it would hurt my family and my siblings.

Chloe and her friend escaped North Korea with the broker, and were passed along to another broker in China to be sold. Chloe's friend was sold as a bride, while Chloe was sold as a domestic slave. Chloe recounted:

> And then we met a broker there. My friend was more mature than me, so my friend was sold to a Chinese man. But nobody bought me because I looked like a kid, like a girl. So, I was not sold to a Chinese man. But the broker sold me to a family who had a son with mental illness. So, I had to take care of the kid.

When discussing evil, Chloe did not discuss her specific experience with trafficking, but rather the entire trafficking industry in general.

Innocence echoed Chloe in viewing the entire trafficking industry as evil and de-humanizing. Innocence shared this about human trafficking:

> First of all, people who defect North Korea and go into China, they go in with a mindset "I need to survive." They lose all humanity basically. Most of them are sold, or they sell themselves. Their humanity is lost.

Innocence herself escaped with the help of a broker, but she felt fear of being sold or trafficked. She shared this about her experience:

Evil: A North Korean Christian Refugee Perspective

> I came alone, but I was scared because I was alone, because I had heard that people were sold, human trafficking, and were taken away without anyone knowing, so I was scared about that. In order to be protected against being sold, I had to be extra nice to the broker, and I had to make sure that I wouldn't be taken away. So that process was really hard.

Reflecting on her experience, Innocence stated:

> This is a strange expression, but I was lucky. Lucky that I wasn't sold. I was able to live in that home, the broker's home, for a while. And we were moved to a different place so that we would not get caught by the police. I had to work to make some money, so I worked.

Emily's life was seriously impacted by human trafficking. When Emily escaped with her mother and her sister, her mother was unknowingly sold as a bride to a Chinese man. Emily shared about that experience:

> At the time that we crossed over into the Chinese city there was a good number of North Korean young ladies at the same time that came together. And a lot of them were there as mail-order brides for the Chinese men. So, the Chinese men would come to them and pay them money. So, my mom was one of those who was sold to a Chinese man. So, my younger sister and I were too young, so we could not be sold.

I asked if Emily's mother had knowingly entered into this situation in order to help her family escape, and Emily clarified:

> No, we didn't know about this. That is just what happened. What my sister and I understood was after our mom had made enough money she would be able to come back and take us, but that was not what happened.

For more than eight years Emily and her sister tried to find their mother. Eventually, they came to believe that their mother had abandoned them, and grew to hate their mother. Emily shared about her experience:

> So, during that time I was actually thinking that our mom had abandoned us. So, I actually really didn't like my mom, we hated my mom. So, when we were coming to Korea that was the thinking we had in our mind. When we came to Korea we resolved that if we end up meeting our mom in Korea we would pretend that we did not know her. So that was the mindset that we had. Even

Findings

> the eight years we were in China we put out through broadcasting or through various channels to try to find our mom. Because we couldn't find her we went ahead and came out to South Korea. We thought maybe there was a possibility that our mom was already in South Korea, but we were told, "No, we didn't get any information." When me and my younger sister were settling in Korea we both resolved that even if mom shows up we will just pretend we don't know her, that she doesn't exist. It had been about twelve or thirteen years since we had been separated from our mom, so we couldn't even remember her face. I had thought if my mom were to come in front of me I would not recognize her.

Then, when they were in South Korea, thirteen years after being separated from their mother, they found out their mother was alive and were reunited through the South Korean government.

Emily remembered:

> Up to the point in [year] I had hated my mom. But in March I suddenly began praying for my mom. And I was surprised: why all of a sudden am I thinking about my mom? So, I began praying for my mom and about two weeks passed and the phone call came from the government center. So, on this phone call they said that, "The description that you gave of your mom, a similar person has entered our government facility."

After several phone calls of information sharing, they believed that they found their mother and set up a meeting. Emily shared about this encounter, saying:

> When we met her, I realized that this really is my mom, and I began to remember what she looked like and knew it was my mom. It was amazing, incredible. At that time, I could share all the things we hated our mom for and all the things we wondered about. We said, "What did you do in these past times?" And then we could all understand and share and our mom explained to us. So, something that was impossible for me to understand I could now understand and it made sense.

Emily and her sister have been working on reconnecting with their mother after being separated for many years. Emily shared the struggle of trying to reconnect after so being separated for so long:

> After my mom finished her time at the government detention center and moved over to do the Hanawon orientation then we went

> back to see my mom one more time. Because we had been apart for so long, at first, we didn't have that closeness. All my mom could recall was when me and my sister were very young. That was March that she came out of Hanawon. We met together after she was released, and it was actually uncomfortable and hard to fit together because of that long distance apart, and my mom had a different memory of me and my sister. So, there was not much closeness and some misunderstanding when we were talking. We had to become familiar with one another again. At first, I confess that I was naughty, I was not polite at first. This is something that can't really be helped, you can't really help this situation. So, then my thinking was I'll just have to accept this for as this is. Instead of thinking like "This is my mom," my thinking adjusted to "This is a person to grow in love for and to adjust to." And now we've gotten a little closer and the situation is a little better.

Emily and her mother and sister meet somewhat regularly to try to re-establish their relationship. After sharing about the story of finding her mother, Emily reflected on the goodness of Christians in her family's story, saying:

> Thinking about my mom, the way she got to come out to South Korea was through some Christian missionaries. But my mom doesn't believe. These days I try to tell my mom, "It's because of the help and kindness of believers that we have been able to be okay and to live well up to now." Right now, my mom doesn't have faith, but when she does come up to Seoul we try to encourage her to have faith and try to invite her to church.

While they all had shared traumatic experiences, Emily and her sister became Christians, while their mother has not.

While most participants highlighted the evil of human traffickers, Miracle's experience of seeing the public execution of human traffickers caused her to feel compassion for them. Miracle shared:

> Like, I felt sorry about them. The government's purpose was that people hate them, and people become frightened by the occasion, but as a kid, looking at them, I felt like they were so sorry, and I felt compassion about them. And I felt disgusting. So, I couldn't have a meal for a couple of days. Because I remembered, you know?

Miracle's encounter with the human traffickers elicited a response of hatred for the government, and not the traffickers.

Findings

Evil of Sexual Violations

In discussing evil events or descriptions of evil, five female participants referenced sexual violations or sexual violence. Each of their stories were about women being abused by men.

Chloe recounted seeing the oppression of vulnerable North Korean women in China:

> There are lots of North Korean women in China who are sold by brokers. I saw North Korean girls working in the adult entertainment industry. And Chinese men and Chinese Korean men make use of them a lot. It's so easy for the men to hit the women and to force them to do whatever they say, even sexual violence. By saying, "What can do you? Even if I hit you, you can't ask the police to help you." So North Korean women in China were beaten a lot by them.

Chloe continued describing the evil of sexual violence against North Korean refugees by telling the story of a woman who had failed a suicide attempt, "I saw another North Korean woman with a lot of scars on her vein [shows wrist], like she cut her vein to die."

In Chloe's eyes, the sexual exploitation of the vulnerable North Korean refugees was the worst evil she witnessed, stating, "Even for the girls who were married. Because there is a lot of violence. So, I think this is the most terrible evil."

Chloe used that event to explain how she began to understand the distinction between good and evil, which she described in terms of human actions based on their belief in God. Chloe said regarding seeing sexual violence:

> I could see how much evil people can do living in the world, in the society, who don't believe in God. On the other hand, I also have experienced people who believe in Jesus, and who are in God, and care about God. So, I can experience the difference between people who believe in God and non-Christians. By looking at that situation it made me believe in evil.

When I asked Chloe her thoughts on those men in China abusing the North Korean girls, she simply replied, "I just feel that they are trashy." I asked Chloe her thoughts about God in light of the abuse she saw in China, and she had this to share:

Evil: A North Korean Christian Refugee Perspective

> I'm not sure if God created that situation. But through that experience there is evil. And nowadays there is a lot of evil and violence in the world, and people do not care about those kinds of things. So, I believe through my experience, what I saw in China, God showed me how evil the world is right now.

For Chloe, the sexual violence she saw in China was one way that God showed her evil in the world.

Eve also heard stories of the sexual abuse of North Korean refugee women in China, which was associated with human trafficking. When first asked about an evil event, Eve recalled, "While staying in China I heard a lot of things about violations happening by Chinese people and by brokers. Such as sexual violations and human trafficking."

Eve highlighted the fact that the brokers who would sell the women into sex trafficking were fellow North Koreans, saying:

> Among the brokers there are North Koreans. Even though they are North Koreans they sell women to Chinese guys without informing them beforehand. They say, "Oh I am going to send you to South Korea, I will help you come to South Korea," but yeah, they just do human trafficking.

When asked about her feelings about the human traffickers, Eve was very clear in her opinion, stating, "I hate those sellers. I pray that those things would never happen again. I was shocked about learning about the real life of North Korean women in China. I feel a lot of compassion for the women."

Emily shared three experiences of what she described as evil, one of which was a graphic recounting of her and her sister's experience of sexual molestation at the hands of a fellow North Korean refugee. They had recently escaped North Korea and were receiving help from a Christian orphanage home while hiding in the mountains. Emily shared about her experience:

> At first when we got out, because we didn't have any identity papers or passports or identification, my younger sister and I had to go live in the mountains inside a tent. This was in the winter time. I was turning 10 and my younger sister was nine, almost 10. So, at the Chinese home there was a young man who was working there; he was also a North Korean refugee. That North Korean boy took food from the Chinese home and brought it out for me and my sister at the tent for every meal. In North Korea they don't

give sex education. So even though we were nine and 10 we didn't know anything about that. One night, even though we said we didn't want to and we didn't know, he was forcibly touching us. So, we kept saying "No! No! We don't want to!" Particularly to my younger sister this North Korean man approached her.

When asked about the frequency of these sexual assaults, she stated that they happened "almost daily." Emily and her sister were too young to understand what was happening, but they knew that they did not want it to happen and resisted. Emily shared, "Because we didn't know anything, we said, 'No we don't want that.' And he said, 'If you say no and don't let me I will stop bringing you food.'"

Despite the threats of withholding food, Emily explained that she and her sister figured out a way to avoid the sexual assault. Emily explained:

> One way we coped was we kind of knew the time when the boy would bring the food. My sister and I would climb up into the mountains to escape. At that time the main feeling we had was scared, fear. We didn't understand.

Emily then explained that she later understood those events as sexual molestation, saying "So, as we started going to school and we started to learn about sex education I began to understand what that was. So, I began to realize that was sexual molestation."

In describing her thoughts about the perpetrator, Emily described him as "really evil," and stated:

> Back then my thought was, wow this person, even though we were that young, that he could do something like that is very bad. So, when I began to understand what was going on I thought that person is really evil.

Emily also highlighted the significance that the perpetrator was a fellow North Korean refugee, and took advantage of other North Korean refugees, saying "Even worse, he's a fellow North Korean refugee, and he could still take advantage of us like that."

Emily shared this story with me through the interpreter, who is her mentor, in a crowded coffee shop of her choosing. I was surprised at her candor, considering the content of the story and the location, but I bracketed my surprise and only displayed empathy and compassion. While she did not demonstrate any emotion while sharing this traumatic story, after the interview with Emily I made sure she had access to free counseling services if needed.

Jane chose to escape North Korea without using a broker specifically so that she would not experience any sexual violations. Jane shared:

> I decided alone to escape with my friends. I said to my friend, "Do you want to escape with me to South Korea for our best future?" She just agreed with me, so then, "Okay let's go." And we didn't use any broker. Because using broker means that I could I have to sell my body.

Jane assumed this risk of escaping without a broker after she had already been imprisoned for a failed escape attempt.

Evil of Discrimination

Six participants spoke of experiencing discrimination which they described as evil. Some participants recounted experiencing discrimination in South Korea at the hands of South Koreans, while others experienced discrimination in China at the hands of Chinese.

Paul experienced discrimination after claiming asylum in South Korea at the hands of a South Korean man, which was his answer to a question about experiencing an evil event.

Paul said about his experience:

> I was talking with my friend on a subway station. I hadn't been in South Korea for much time, so I still used a North Korean accent a little bit. And an old man who looked like a gentleman asked me where I was from. So, I didn't say anything. And then the gentleman asked me again one more time, "Where are you from? Are you from China?" So, I said "No." And then I felt like weird and looked back and the old man was staring at me. And then when the old man was getting off of the train he stepped on my toes, on my feet. So, as I was not yet adjusted to South Korean culture at that time I felt [that I was receiving] ignorant treatment from that man. Just treating me like I was a Chinese-Korean. So, I decided to change my accent and the intonation of my language. That was the worst time for me.

Paul reflected on what he learned through that event—that people have biases in this world, and that humans are all created in the image of God. Paul explained his thoughts:

Findings

> Some people have an interest in North Koreans. But the others have strong bias towards defectors. But in the vision of God I think he creates people all the same as me. They're all what the Creator made. Through that instance I decided to change my accent. On the other hand, I shouldn't be like that old man. I shouldn't have any bias or prejudice against someone like him.

Paul then stated that he believed all North Koreans in South Korea felt vulnerable to discrimination, stating, "In South Korea the North Koreans have an inferiority complex. It just feels like someone might discriminate against me in society."

Gideon's mother left South Korea and moved to the United States because of the discrimination she experienced. Gideon described with enthusiasm how much his mother prefers to live in the United States:

> Yeah, she really loves the States! Because when she was in South Korea, you know her accent is really different from South Korean. So, some people ask my mom, "Where are you from?" She felt very stressful about that. She would have to explain to every person she met. That's why she didn't like South Korea.

Gideon's mother experiences anonymity in the United States, which she prefers to the othering she experienced in South Korea. Gideon shared about his mother's experience:

> But after she went to the States, if someone asks her "Where are from?" she'll just say, "I'm from Korea," or they say, "Oh, Asian." They don't distinguish North and South Korean or China or anywhere; they just distinguish her as Asian. And she likes it. And also, from the beginning she loved the States. She wanted to live there. That's why she always tells me to move to the United States.

Faith also commented on discrimination towards North Koreans that can be found in South Korea, usually in online forums. Faith had this to say about discrimination:

> I think people don't say that to your face, but they do that behind you. So, it's not talking about me specifically, I feel that because I see the comments on the articles. So, every time something happens in North Korea there will be an article on the internet and I click into it, and there are a lot of comments saying 'ah go back to North Korea. Why are you here? I didn't ask you come to South Korea.' There are a bunch of comments like that.

Evil: A North Korean Christian Refugee Perspective

Faith also reads comments on these forums in support of North Koreans, recalling:

> I mean there are still a lot of people saying, "Ah North Korean pity. We have to help them. How would you feel if you were born in North Korea? They're just unlucky. You didn't do anything right that deserved to be born in South Korea." So, there's so many good people like that, nice people.

Regardless of the comments of support, Faith believes the discriminatory comments towards North Koreans are unfair, and they hurt her feelings. She shared her feelings, saying:

> But still, a few comments, or those kind of bad comments hurts my feelings. No matter how many good people there are. But I didn't choose to be born in North Korea. It's not my fault. We were all in the same root; we're all the same ethnic. So, in the Korean War, some people had to go to war. And who knows? Maybe sometime my grandfather was originally born in South Korea, and he has to go to war in the North. Is that fair? No, it's not.

Ultimately, Faith understands why there is discrimination against North Koreans, even if she disagrees with them. Faith explained:

> So, yes. But I understand, I know why they are saying that. This is their country, they are the land owner, they were here from the beginning. But suddenly the North Koreans came and took away the advantages, takes advantage of this country. So, I know how they feel.

Some participants spoke of North Korean refugees experiencing discrimination in China. Eve, Emily, and Chloe all witnessed North Korean women experiencing discrimination, which were all highlighted under the human trafficking and sexual violation sections. Innocence experience discrimination firsthand while in China. Innocence shared:

> But it was hard living there even for that short time because I was discriminated against; not treated properly, looked down on. There was no one to protect me, so I needed to protect myself, take care of myself. I had to continually humble myself, disregard myself. And all the money that I earned, the broker took that money. So, when I left China to journey into South Korea I had to be very careful, and I was also afraid something would happen to me.

When I asked how and why she was discriminated against, Innocence told me:

> Where I stayed in China was a village, a countryside. And they know the people that come from North Korea. They know, "Oh that person is from North Korea." . . . Because they are known, for all the North Koreans to come over, to be sold. To some kind of work or situation. So, they just think of them as people that are sold into human trafficking or labor. Most of the people who are sold are from a very poor family, so when you come over from North Korea they just assume you are very poor and uneducated.

The discrimination was not solely from non-North Koreans towards North Koreans. When asked to discuss an evil event that she experienced, Innocence highlighted the time when her fellow North Koreans treated her like an "outsider." She recounted:

> Growing up, my parents always taught me that you should help people and people will help you. But when I came out into the real world, it wasn't so. Especially the North Koreans who defected; the broker was a North Korean, and North Koreans are so angry and bitter inside, the ones who have defected, and they only look out for themselves. And they do a lot of bad and evil things to protect themselves and only do good for themselves. And so, helping others and to see that was really hard, because that was different from what I was taught by my parents.

Innocence was abandoned by her fellow North Korean broker in China, leaving her alone to figure out how to make the journey to Thailand. Her abandonment was referenced as another example of evil that she experienced in her life. She shared her story of being abandoned with me:

> I was introduced to this broker in North Korea by someone I knew. And this broker is not a broker who brings people into South Korea, or helps them to defect to South Korea. This broker's job is to help them find work in China. So, my goal was to go to China to find work. My goal was not to defect and come to South Korea. The reason I came to South Korea was after I went into China, I was with the broker lady, but in our process of moving around the broker got a message from her husband to meet with him, so the broker just left me in the middle of nowhere in China. So, I had nothing, I had no money. I couldn't go back to North Korea, so I decided to come back to South Korea.

Innocence felt betrayed by the way the broker, a fellow North Korean, abandoned her. Later in the interview, Innocence also contrasted the way she was raised by her parents with the way North Koreans treat each other in China. She explained:

> In North Korea, my dad was a doctor, when people were ill or sick or bleeding to death my dad would go out and help them or bandage them. And he would come home very happy that he was able to help others; that was the kind of life that we lived. . . . But when people defect they become totally different people. . . . The kind of life I lived in North Korea I tried in China. But when I did, I was taken advantage of, I was persecuted. I was betrayed.

The discrimination that Innocence experienced at the hands of her fellow North Korean refugees in China impacted the way she knew how to live life. She shared:

> So, when those things happened to me I began to change my mind. I began to change the way I started living my life, "I can't live in a naïve way like this." I began to not trust people, and not live the kind of life I lived in North Korea.

Innocence's experience highlighted how discrimination experienced by the North Korean refugees was not limited to outsiders, but included other refugees as well.

Evil as Spiritual Oppression

In addition to government actions, human trafficking, sexual violations, and discrimination, one participant, Gideon, also discussed evil in terms of spiritual oppression.

Gideon recounted a personal experience with a demonic attack as an example of evil that happened in his own life. Gideon shared:

> Last year I slept and I had a dream. At that dream I saw the devil. I didn't think the devil was really horrible, I just read the Word that said, "Oh he's horrible, he's horrible." I previously didn't feel fear. But in that dream, I saw the devil; I don't know if it was the devil or not, but for me it was very, very horrible. It was the most horrible dream; it was really a nightmare. So, when I woke up, I prayed to God. I didn't know the meaning of the devil, but I saw it in the dream. And it was really horrible that I couldn't fight against it. But I was lucky to pray to God about that. So, I said,

Findings

"Oh my God, I'm not ready to fight against the devil," because it was very, very horrible.

I asked Gideon what the devil in his dream looked like, and he expounded upon his experience:

> It was similar to people, to humans. But when I saw his eyes, it was very black. No white, just black. And I felt it just looked like a black hole. My everything was getting pulled in to it, and the devil didn't do anything. He just saw me. And when I made eye contact with him I felt very horrible and I couldn't do anything.

The experience of his nightmare has left a lasting impact on Gideon, especially in regards to the power of evil forces. He shared:

> And also, until now I remember the feeling. So, I always think that the devil is much more dangerous and has greater black power than we expect. But I can't say it was the devil 100 percent, but in my life, it was the worst horrible nightmare and the worst dream.

I asked Gideon if he had any waking examples of evil that he could think of. He immediately began discussing the activities of cults in South Korea. Gideon believed the way cults ruined people's lives evil. He stated:

> And also, I've seen many people go to cult churches. It's not church. It's a cult organization, and they give all of their money and their everything. And then the cult organization they ruin people's lives. And I think it's really the worst evil.

Gideon then recounted two experiences he had with cults in South Korea, concluding with stating that those experiences were "evil."

The participants in this study described evil in light of the fallenness of humanity as a power dynamic where the powerful oppressed or took advantage of the vulnerable. The powerful actors were all considered to be human beings or human institutions, while one participant also added the actions of spiritual or demonic forces as actors as well.

SOVEREIGNTY OF GOD

In discussing the sovereignty of God, nine participants mentioned the "plan" that God has for people in general or for North Korea specifically. Seven out of the twelve participants discussed God's plan in terms of specific or personal plans for individual people. Additionally, five participants expressed questions or doubts about God's sovereignty. In this section I will first share the findings regarding the participants' thoughts on God's plan. I will then share the questions and doubts that participants expressed about God's sovereignty.

God's Plan

Innocence stated that when she thinks about God's plan "I feel that God is reliable. . . . Because I believe that God is good, God will always protect me and will not harm me." Emily's perspective on God has changed as she has grown in her Christian faith, particularly in regards to God's plan in the midst of hardship. Emily explained her perspective:

> In the past I asked that and wondered why it was. And also, why do only these kinds of things happen to me? Why? As I think back to that, well that was before I believed in God and some of it was from my limited perspective, and it was my own choice and selfish desire.

Emily still has times when she asks God why she is experiencing hardships. She shared:

> Even nowadays when things are difficult I might ask "God, why? Why? Why are you giving me this hardship or this temptation?" But now I have a different perspective. I ask, "God, what is your purpose in these hardships or temptations?"

Emily's perspective has begun to change from asking God why things are happening to asking God what His plan is through certain difficulties. She explained:

> Now my perspective is when it's difficult is, "God, what is your plan, and how are you going to work through these situations?" These days I am seeking God's plan and what he would want me to do. The question changed from "why" to "what is your plan, and what do you want me to work through this?"

Similar to Emily, Faith has progressed from asking God why she was experiencing difficulties to trusting that God has a plan in the midst of it. Previously Faith would blame God for her difficulties. She shared, "I blame God. 'Oh, why are those non-believers having a good life? They're living so happily, and why do I have to go through all that difficulties?' So, I blame God." Faith has noticed a pattern, however, when she looks back at her life, and sees God's purpose through difficulties. She shared:

> But nowadays I am trying not to blame so much. Because every time I look back I understand, "Okay that was a plan." "Okay that was the plan." So, this repeats so many times I think, 'Oh, am I too dumb to experience the same thing over and over and still blame God?" So, I try not to. I pray, I say, "Oh God, okay from now on I will try not to blame. And even though you didn't listen to my prayer, I will try to trust in You, I will try to not blame You too much." So, I'm trying.

Ultimately, Faith does not seek out further difficulties, but does trust that any hardships she encounters are part of God's plan to produce growth in her. She explained:

> But to God. I don't know what to say. I just feel like, oh, I didn't choose that, and God has a plan, and if he has a plan, I have no way but to follow. Again, all the difficulties I have experienced is part of the plan that God has, so okay, that will make me stronger and will make me grow and become a better person. After I have overcome all those difficulties I think it's okay; I'm not hoping I have any other challenges.

Faith later continued, "Also, because I have looked back at my life a lot and always concluded okay if that didn't happen I wouldn't be who I am now." In summarizing her thoughts on the experiences of her life, Faith simply stated, "Yes, but for the past. I'm grateful."

I was struck by the depth of trust that Faith has in God, despite the experiences and struggles she faced. I asked Faith what may have influenced her thoughts on God's plan for her life. Faith shared that her thoughts were influenced by her Christian faith, stating, "I think because I am a believer. I am exposed to the Bible, the Christian environment. So, I read the Bible, my pastor preaches a lot." The biblical story of Joseph is particularly significant for her. Faith shared:

> Especially I think Joseph's story inspires me a lot. So, every time I read about that story. Joseph, he was the beloved son. But he was sent to Egypt and lived as a slave. That's so miserable. If I were Joseph I would be like, "Ugh, my life is down. I'm not going to live." I don't know. But he was in that situation, and he still tried to do his best for everything, like doing the servant work. And when the woman tempts him, he is always so good, I think that comes from his faith.

Evil: A North Korean Christian Refugee Perspective

In addition to the Bible, Faith's mother has influenced her own views on the plans of God for their lives. Faith said this about her mother's influence on her life:

> Also, I talk a lot to my mom, like my mom and I have a lot of conversations. So, every time we recall our memory we say, "Oh yes! Yes! That's why this happened. Oh, let's be thankful." So, she says a lot like that, so I think that's probably why.

While Emily and Faith had begun to ask a different question to God amid difficulties,

Candice felt that her journey to South Korea was God's plan for her life, in spite of her own desires. Candice professed:

> When I was young I believed I would live well in China. However, if the others had persuaded me to come to South Korea, I would not be persuaded by them. At that time, I was so stubborn. I was too stubborn to be persuaded by others. That's why the pastors made the plan without my will, my choice. And I believe it was God's will for me.

Candice then clarified she believed that she was so stubborn that being sent to China and then sent against her knowledge to South Korea was the way God brought her to where she is today.

Likewise, Gideon believed it was God's plan to bring him out of North Korea to South Korea. Gideon shared this about his belief:

> But totally when I looked back at my life and my experience from North Korea to South Korea to the States, I don't think it was made naturally. He planned it, and he has a reason for me to escape North Korea and the first time I saw the church, it was the beginning that I started to believe in God. So, he led me to this position.

Gideon went on to explain his belief that God has a plan for his future, particularly in regards to North and South Korea. He explained:

> But in the future, I think he has a plan that I have to do something for Him. Especially related to North Korea. Because he needs people who can deal with North Korea, who know North Korea and South Korea well. So, I think, I guess, he will use me in that kind of position in the future.

Gideon further elaborated that he believes God's plan for his life includes telling North Koreans about God, saying:

> But one thing is clear for me; I always think I want to tell my experience about God to North Koreans too. That's why he wanted that part for me. Because if South Koreans explain God to the North Korean people, they don't know the North Korean people's life. And it's not easy to explain God to North Koreans, because they live a totally different life. Especially a person who came from North Korea who believes in God, they can share their experience. And from that way, God can let North Koreans believe in God, through each other.

Of all the participants, Jane stood out as having a unique view of God's plan, using the language of force. She explained her thoughts, saying:

> Okay, when I was a little girl I didn't know about God, and after I escaped from North Korea I didn't know about Him, but now as I am thinking about Him, North Korea government doesn't like God. So, I think that maybe God forced them to escape from North Korea, and forced them to destroy their selves. I think something like that.

I asked Jane to clarify what she meant by saying that God was forcing the North Korean government to destroy itself. She highlighted the government's economic management of the country, but again used the language of force. She said:

> I think God forced them to, it's kind of a chain. God forced them to destroy the country themselves. They are just selling whatever. For example, if you have some valuable resources and then you change them with some bread, that's a crazy thing. But that's exactly what North Korea does, it's an isolated country. They are forced to do this. God made it like that. . . . But they sell cheaply and that means that they just destroy themselves. And I mean everything works just through God.

Jane expressed her belief that everything works through God, including some countries being ravaged by COVID-19. Jane had this to say concerning COVID-19:

> The Earth just goes always. And something happening to another country, like Coronavirus, like for us that was a big disease. I think people can't control that. Some countries are just destroyed, and it was I think included in God's work.

I was interested in what made Jane think that, as it was different from what other participants expressed. Jane told me:

Evil: A North Korean Christian Refugee Perspective

> Actually, we are Christians and we go to church, but because of Coronavirus we can't go to church, but we can worship online. And we hear some kinds of sermons online and some of the sermons say it like that. But I agree with them. Because as we read the Bible we can think like that way. . . . And also, I feel that way because everything God just has control of on Earth. He made everything. As we can see in the Bible some words that God says everything is through me and is happening like that.

Jane's firm belief in God's plan also extends to her own life and salvation, which she explained through saying "God chose me. . . . I didn't choose him." She later continued:

> The Earth just moves, right? So, it's just a plan. Without a plan everything doesn't work at all. It can't work at all. Yeah, so if he doesn't have any plan for us and then maybe I couldn't be here, I shouldn't be here. Correctly I should be in Hell now. That's right.

Jane also placed her hope in God's plan for the future of North and South Korea. She expressed her hopes for a unified Korea, saying:

> I think God's thinking and planning is incredible, just incredible. I can't even imagine about it. I think, I believe, hopefully God will save our country as soon as possible. Because they [we] can be unified, South, and North. Like Germany. Yeah, some day.

Some participants echoed Jane's belief that God has specific plans for North Korea. Gideon believed that North Koreans have a special place in the task of world evangelism, stating:

> I believe North Koreans live a very difficult life and a very special life. More than South Korea or any other countries in the world. They have a very special experience. So, from those people can be a seed to spread real Christians to China and Russia and Asia and to all around the world.

Like Gideon, Ruth also believed God's plan for North Koreans to participate in the expansion of the Gospel. Ruth said, "Also, through the defectors God has helped to save the country. Someday God will lead the country, people will lead the country to freedom to save the country. Also, the Bible and Gospel can be spread to North Koreans."

Findings

Questions and Doubts about the Sovereignty of God

Some participants discussed having questions or doubts about the sovereignty of God in light of evil in the world. Four participants shared their doubts during the interview process. Miracle expressed a belief in the sovereignty of God, while also questioning why God does not intervene in some circumstances. She reflected on a recent news story that she described as "evil" about a mother and daughter who were found murdered, and said:

> It is not the society that God wants for us, I think. Also, it's written in the Bible, "Don't kill anybody," like that, so, of course, it's horrible. But, it's really kind of like a kid's question, but I always think like, "If God knows everything, in this case, how, you know, what if God stops him [the murderer] being like that, because he knows everything." That is my question.

The question Miracle asked is about the interaction between human actions and God's omniscience and sovereignty in light of evil. Miracle did not express any type of answer to her question, but let it stand unanswered.

Gideon wondered why God does not intervene in unfair situations. Reflecting on his own life, Gideon asked:

> So that's why I have a question why there are always unfair situations in our life. And especially why do North Koreans have to suffer from the North Korean government. Especially my life, why would you [God] let me be born in North Korea and have lots of bad experiences and horrible experiences compared with South Koreans? I had lots of questions about that.

Gideon's questions were not answered per se, but he did express an understanding that things happen due to God's purpose. He shared:

> But finally, I didn't find the real answer, but I was able to understand. There is God's purpose. And unfair situations, I imagine if everyone is clever and intelligent, we couldn't make our world. Because I think there are various things in our lives; someone is really good at art, or someone is really good at science. I admitted it.

In Gideon's reflection about people having different abilities, he came to an understanding that life is not always fair, and thus some people will be born in better situations that others. However, Gideon believes that God still has His specific purpose for Gideon's life, which involves him living in South Korea.

Evil: A North Korean Christian Refugee Perspective

Faith, like Gideon, expressed some questions about why God allows North Korea to continue to be led by the regime. When discussing the government of North Korea, Faith said, "So, at a young age I wondered why would God leave those leaders on the Earth? Why doesn't God take them to the hell? But, okay, that's God's choice. I have nothing to say about that. So, whatever."

Faith indicated that she asked that question when she was younger, so I asked what her current thoughts were. She shared:

> I'm not asking anymore, but I'm still hoping that something happens. Still hoping "Okay please, I hope that reunification comes true." Okay maybe it's not reunification, but at least people from North and South they can commute. Like traveling is okay—I hope that happens. And I hope that the government can change in other ways. I hope someone else becomes another leader. A reasonable person.

I asked Faith if her North Korean friends ask that question as well, and she replied that she was not sure because she does not ask them about those questions. However, she then shared, "I can see some people are still asking the question and some people are like me, but the one thing is that we all hope that North Korea becomes better." Faith has moved on from asking her question without answering it, but instead places her focus on hope for the future.

Job's experience in North Korea left him with several doubts about God's plan, and by extension, God's character. Job shared his thoughts:

> When I first came to church and began to believe in God little by little I used to hear that God is in peace and in love. But bringing back the memories I experienced in North Korea, I matched that situation with the personality of God; it didn't match well. It made me think that "God is cruel, he's not merciful." And people, especially South Korea people, they say easily about the situation happening in North Korea, "Even that situation is in the way of God's planning, God's providence." But could you say that easily like that if it was your story, or your experience? So, I started feeling skepticism about God, and that God might have two sides, good and cruel.

I wanted to know if Job still believed that God had two sides. He shared in response:

> Actually, my thought on the two sides of God has decreased while going to church and believing in God deeper and deeper. Also, in the Bible we can see so many stories, like worse things happened in the Bible. For example, Abraham had to offer his only kid to God when God asked. Also, Jonah. And Paul who had to go to Rome to spread the Gospel, even though he was in a dangerous situation. Also, Job in the Bible. So, it's hard to understand all the things God leads and makes. So, it's the same for understanding the situation in North Korea as well. However, it's still difficult for me to understand the situations in North Korea that I witnessed when I was younger.

Reading the Bible has helped Job with trusting God and His plan, but he still finds it difficult to understand God's sovereignty.

I asked Job a follow up question about God's providence, as he was clearly upset when he mentioned what he had been told in South Korea. Job responded:

> Talking about God's providence makes me angry and upset. Because South Koreans know nothing about the real situation, the terrible things happening in North Korea. So, saying just like this makes me upset. All these terrible situations are happening, such as political prison camps, public executions, and living without any protection of law and human rights violations. South Koreans know nothing about this situation because they live in a better situation and a better society. So, to say it like that, that it is God's providence, might be easy for them.

Job then expressed his opinion on how the discussion of God's providence might keep North Koreans from attending church. He shared his opinion:

> Sometimes in South Korean church, the members of the church are so dedicated to spread the Gospel to North Koreans, they say to North Koreans, "Oh, thanks to the help of God you could come to South Korea! He led you to South Korea. And it's his grace." I don't think that's a good way to say to them as soon as they visit the church. Because it might cause them to leave the church and it might cause them to have borders in their mind against South Koreans or against the church.

Even though Job still does not understand God's providence in light of what he experienced in North Korea, he still sees God working very personally in his life. Immediately following his opinions on God's sovereignty, he then shared a more recent story where he said he heard the voice of God:

Evil: A North Korean Christian Refugee Perspective

> I recently prayed, "God, please let me attend early morning prayer at least three times." . . . On that day when I was going to give up going to early morning prayer I heard an auditory hallucination, like God said, "Just go with the belief. God will allow you to go there."

I wanted to clarify if Job thought he was hallucinating, or if he heard the voice of God, and he replied:

> I believe it was God. I heard exactly, "Get out of here by faith." So, the next day I attended early morning prayer with joy. When my mom found out I was going to early morning prayer she said, "Are you crazy? You have to go to work after finishing early morning prayer! How can you wake up? How can you overcome all the heavy workload at your job?" But when I attended the early morning prayer I felt like I could overcome the limits in my life with the help of God. God gives me the power and energy and ability to overcome the limits. So, I messaged my mom saying, "It's just the advantage in my life, because I can overcome the limits in this period. It will help me to change my life as well." And I stopped smoking going to early morning prayer.

Job, in responding to questions where he expressed doubts about God's character and sovereignty, ended his sharing with this most recent story by sharing how God has been changing his life for the better. While Job never directly answered his questions, he pivoted to reflecting and sharing on how God is working and active in his life.

GOODNESS OF GOD

All the participants expressed a belief in the goodness of God. Participants spoke of gratitude towards God and described God as a God who answers prayers. Two major themes about the goodness of God that emerged were the belief that God loves North Koreans, and the belief that God is just in his judgment.

God Who Loves North Koreans

Eight of the participants spoke of understanding God as a God who loves North Koreans. Participants expressed their understanding of God's heart for North Korea in terms of God's thoughts and actions for North Korea.

Faith, speaking on the relationship between God and North Koreans, simply stated, "God loves them." When I asked Faith about a time when she knew that God was good, she shared a remarkable testimony. She was initially afraid that I would not believe her, but when I assured her that I trusted her, she shared again about the time when her mother was sent back to North Korea:

> Ah, yes please, because it might sound kind of superstitious. So, when I was young, my mom, she was sent to North Korea when she was in China. So back then my younger sister and I were with my stepfather. So, we were staying without my mom. So, one day, I just dreamed a number, and in the dream it says, "On this date my mom is going to come back to China." And then I was like, "Oh what was that number? What was that number?" And then I just had a feeling that my mom was going to come back for us. And that came true. I don't exactly remember if that date is correct, but anyways very soon my mom came back to us. So, I decided, "Okay I will trust God."

When Faith saw that I did not doubt her story, she continued on:

> So if that didn't happen, I might think, "Oh okay, maybe I was just lucky enough." But that one, the dream I had. . . . And it's not the only event. I had several experiences of dreaming something. Another time was I dreamed my stepfather was, he got in a car accident. So, there was a car accident with my stepfather, and that was in my dream as well. It wasn't too serious, he was ok, but the fact that he was in that accident was true. So, things like this. So, ok, if there is no God, that wouldn't happen.

I asked Faith if she often has dreams like this, and she told me that they happened when she was younger but not as much now. I asked her why she thought she does not dream like that anymore and she said, "Nowadays, maybe my life is too peaceful." She went on to clarify:

> I mean, peaceful enough. Not "too" peaceful. Right. . . . Because dreaming is the easier way for me to feel something. Because these days I have time, I'm able to read the Bible. But back then I was too young, there was no way for me to begin reading the Bible initially.

For Faith, the goodness of God was exemplified in her receiving messages in her dreams when she was unable to learn about Him through other means.

When discussing God and North Korea, Innocence had a response that highlighted the caring nature of God, stating:

Evil: A North Korean Christian Refugee Perspective

> I don't know if I can express it in a very theological or religious way... but if I were to express it, God is always mindful of North Korea. That he is always looking at North Korea and is mindful of North Korea.

Ruth echoed Innocence's comments, saying, "I believe that God will always think about North Koreans and will work for the country for North Koreans."

Paul discussed the goodness of God in a more personal way, sharing how God has been good in his life:

> Almost every single day I appreciate God for everything. I brought nothing from North Korea, but as I have a house and the necessary things for living, and for every single thing I have I feel grateful. Especially as I realize the limits of my efforts I can see God allows me to do what I want.

Paul was the only participant to discuss God's love for not just himself or the North Korean population, but for the governmental leaders as well. Concerning the government of North Korea, Paul stated:

> I believe that God accepts the right person and the cruel person as well. And God waits for them to confess and realize their sins. God wants that they might believe someday and realize Christianity and confess what they did to people.

Candice, however, felt that God had already begun to punish the Kim regime, because of the brokenness of Kim Jong Eun's family, exemplified in the assassination of Kim Jong Eun's brother.

When I asked Gideon about a time when he thought that God is good, he immediately responded with retelling his escape story:

> Gideon: The first time I met Him. The first time the pastor helped us, I thought he was a good person and he helped us, but later I thought that of course the pastor was a good person, but God helped us through him. We couldn't find any other home. We were at the edge of the, how do you say, hill?
>
> Ryan: You were at the edge of the cliff?
>
> Gideon: Yes. We couldn't find any other way, and God was the only way we were able to survive. But he helped us, he rescued us.

For Gideon, God protected and rescued him and his mother from North Korea, which exemplified God's goodness.

Findings

Innocence, like Gideon, described God as a rescuer. When discussing her feelings about God when she was abandoned in China, Innocence stated:

> I didn't know God then when I was with the broker. But to me God is someone who I can cry out to, call out to, when I'm in need; someone that would answer, who will come to rescue me.

Innocence has a very personal understanding of God's character as a rescuer of North Koreans.

God Who Is Just

During the interview process, ten participants discussed the goodness of God in terms of God's just character—that God judges sin and does not punish people unfairly. Several participants discussed hearing explanations for the suffering of North Koreans as God's punishment for the sins of North Korea. While they were told this, all but one of the participants did not believe that God was punishing North Korea.

Innocence, reflecting on the question as to why North Korea is the way it is, stated, "I pray about that every day. If you are North Korean that's the prayer you say every day." I asked her if any pastor had ever tried to give her an answer to that question, and she responded that, "If there was any pastor who had an answer for that I probably wouldn't go to that pastor's church." Innocence has concluded that "Only God knows the answer to that."

Ruth echoed Innocence in both her question of why and her conclusion that only God knows the answer. She expressed her thoughts with these words:

> That's the most common doubt from North Koreans: Why is it different between North Korea and South Korea? Why have North Korean people been forced by the government without freedom? . . . I believe it would be impossible to find the answer of why North Koreans have to overcome lots of bad things.

I asked Ruth if anyone had ever tried to give her an answer to that question. She responded that she had been told by a pastor at her church that the "North Korean people have been abandoned by God." The reason God abandoned North Korea, according to this pastor, is because "the government kills people who believe in God. The people pray and bow to human idols. That's why the country is so poor and bad things happen there, because of that."

The translator, Miracle, then stated that she too has been told that God has abandoned North Korea. I asked Ruth if she believed that God has abandoned North Korea, and she immediately responded, "No. It's the government's fault. The reason people are poor is the money is spent on the military."

Emily had also heard in a sermon that God was punishing North Korea. When I asked her thoughts on that, she agreed with Ruth and Innocence, stating, "I really don't know, because only God knows." She then stated that she did not think asking God why North Korea is suffering is the right question to ask. Emily explained what she believed is the right question to ask:

> For me the right question is, "What is God doing? And what is God calling me to do?" Whether it means to help other people or to help North Korea; how can I obey God and what he is wanting to do? That's where my focus is.

In discussing the idea that God might be punishing North Korea, Emily continued,

> I'm not confident that God has a plan to punish the North. I don't sense that. That's only something that the Lord knows and that's his prerogative, and I can't really say that he will or he will not, but that's not even for me to focus on.

Miracle was a little more descriptive about her questions to God, and expressed some honest complaints to God about North Korea. Miracle confessed:

> Actually, I have lots of complaints to God, thinking about the history I experienced in North Korea. I've asked questions a lot to pastors, like God loves. God is love, you know? And he said in the Bible that he made people, you know, like His image. So then, why doesn't he rescue them from the violent government?

I wanted to know what pastors had told Miracle. She recounted that they said:

> North Koreans have done lots of sins for a long time, so they have been punished. . . . Yes, they made their sins by bowing in front a person; people who don't know about God, but they believe in all the idols in their life.

Miracle then explained how she felt that it was unfair to punish the North Koreans for not knowing about God, saying:

> But that's really unfair, you know? What I think is they didn't throw God away, they didn't know when they were born, I didn't know when I was born about God. Because nobody talks about God in North Korea. The government prevents people from believing in God. Yeah. It's not their fault actually, it's the government's fault. I didn't appreciate that answer the pastors gave.

I found this significant, as Miracle had earlier admitted to feeling guilty herself for bowing before idols in North Korea. I dug a little deeper into what Miracle thought about the situation then in regard to God. She confessed some deep questions that she had when she responded with:

> I am wondering if God really works, God really knows, about all the situations. So, I believe in God, and I feel grateful a lot, and I pray, and I try to become a mature Christian. But whenever thinking of North Korea and Africa, you know, people who are forced and threatened by the government. If God works and knows all the terrible things, why doesn't he rescue them. Why doesn't he work, you know?

Miracle then mentioned that her North Korean friends in South Korea all thought the same way. Miracle shared this regarding her understanding of what her North Korean friends believe:

> Yeah, thinking of their parents and siblings living still in North Korea. Yeah, they're like me. Because, what's not fair is that they don't have any choice in their life. In South Korea, people have choice whether they choose God or not. But people in North Korea don't have any information about Jesus and God. Then, how could it be the same?

Then Miracle asserted that she believed that people who are totally unaware of God should not be held accountable for sins they commit unknowingly. Miracle stated:

> How could they know it was sin? Being unaware of God. It's not their fault. Pastors here say, "Respecting and bowing in front of individual people is sin," but as many customs in North Korea, they don't know about God. I think, "How could you say that?"

Miracle concluded her questions about God's actions in relation to North Korea by questioning his timing, asking:

Evil: A North Korean Christian Refugee Perspective

> When is his time? Pastors always say, "It's not his time, so he doesn't touch them," so when is his time? And how can all the people be compensated for sacrifice, for their death, without really committing any serious crime?

Miracle struggled with the answers she has received from pastors about why North Korea is the way it is. Unlike Innocence, who concluded that only God has the answer, Miracle remains unsatisfied and wants an answer. At this point in the interview, Miracle sat up and used hand gestures, emphatically saying:

> I want to know. I really want to know why North Koreans are punished according to the pastors. Even though it was one country and now its shattered in two; some live in a developed country and some live in a terrible place. And that's unfair. I want to know the answer why it's different.

Even though she wants an answer, Miracle stated that she and her North Korean friends all hate any answer they have been given, again emphatically stating, "They hate the answer that 'North Koreans are punished. North Koreans are punished by God.' They hate that answer." Miracle then sat back in her chair, paused for a moment, and then said, "You know, it is quite cold." Later in the interview, Miracle stated, "People from North Korea are hurt, get hurt from the church by those kinds of answers, you know? They leave church, you know?"

Like Miracle, Gideon admitted to having questions about God's justice concerning the situation in North Korea. He shared, "I also have some questions about God. Why does he allow suffering to the North Korean people? Because they don't even know anything about God." Like Miracle, Gideon believes that the people who are suffering in North Korea are not being judged by God because they do not know about God.

Gideon also struggles with his view that the government has not been punished by God. Gideon shared, "But he didn't punish them. He just let them play in North Korea. He didn't do any other punishment that humans understand. He didn't give any sufferings to the North Korean government." However, Gideon expressed a belief that in the end, the government will be punished, saying, "I think he will show the results about of the North Korean government's conclusion at the end. He knows."

Gideon's trust in God goes beyond what he can comprehend. Gideon said, "But, ah. I think there is a plan we can't understand. I think he planned something for our country, but we are human. I can't understand his purpose." Gideon believes that God has a plan and there is a reason for the suffering of North Koreans.

> But I believe he has a plan, and there is a reason why North Koreans are suffering and also why our country is divided into two parts, North and South. There is God's plan. So, I think he will show the results in the future.

Gideon's trust in God includes a trust in the future.

Faith also stated that she had questions about why North Korea is suffering. She agreed with Miracle and Gideon that God is not punishing North Koreans, and expressed trust that God would be just. Faith responded to the notion that God is punishing North Korea by saying:

> First of all, it hurts my feelings. I don't know. If God is punishing one country, did all the people do something wrong? Why would God just punish one country? I mean South Koreans sin, Americans sin, they all sin, we're all sinners. Why would somebody say that? That's not true.

Faith then shared her thoughts about the suffering in North Korea:

> So, people are suffering there, but it's not because God is angry at them; they didn't do anything that is so wrong. They were just born there. So, the reason they are still in North Korea is because our life is not the end on this earth. So, after we die, we have some other choice. So, for those people, they didn't have a chance to know God, they didn't have the opportunity. So maybe God has other plans: "For the people who didn't get to know me I'll say something else to judge them."

Faith then reiterated the fact that this present life is not all there is, but there is an afterlife as well, which enables her to believe that God is not unfair, stating, "So if I think that life on earth is all what it is, then that's so unfair and so sad, but if you think about after we die there is something else. There is Heaven and Hell."

Job echoed Faith and Miracle, questioning why God would allow such suffering in North Korea, "Before I used to ask God, 'Why do you allow them, the government, to be bad and cruel?'" Job, like Faith, found hope in the goodness of God in the afterlife. He explained his thoughts:

> But recently reading the Bible and the book of Job, the words made me think in different ways. The Lord gives and the Lord takes away. Reading that story, maybe the people who are dead or killed

> by the government will be in Heaven now, and God might have brought them to Heaven because living in Heaven is much better than living in North Korea. So, God might bring them to Heaven because it's unbelievable, it's incredible to understand the terrible things that are happening in North Korea rationally.

Job, while holding the government actions of killing people as terrible, sees God's goodness in those people being brought to Heaven to escape North Korea. In Job's perspective, God is not abandoning North Koreans, but rescuing them into Heaven.

Eve said she has never been told that North Korea has been abandoned by God. She strongly disagreed with the notion, saying:

> God doesn't give us judgment, even though we make lots of sins in our life. And it's Kim Jong Eun and the government who should be judged by God. It's not the citizens living in North Korea. Also, it's God's grace and his plan to rescue North Koreans from North Korea into South Korea so defectors could meet their parents. So, I believe God is rescuing North Koreans from the evil government, and he knows everything.

Eve also said she did not pray to God asking him questions about why North Korea is the way it is. Rather, she said, "My prayers are different. I ask God to end this situation from the Coronavirus, and please help North Koreans to come to South Korea. Please rescue them from that place."

Interestingly, three participants described the relationship between God and North Koreans as analogous to the relationship between God and the Israelites. Specifically, they mentioned the stories of Israel in the desert in Exodus and the Babylonian captivity to explain the current situation in North Korea. When discussing the famine in North Korea, Candice used the time of the Israelites in the desert to explain God's continued providence and care for North Koreans. Candice reflected on the famine in North Korea, saying:

> I think it was God's allowance. For example, the Israel people stayed in the desert for forty years. At that time God provided food for them, but they always complained to God. So, it's the same in North Korea; people always complain about the situation that they face now. They only follow survival and the things to survive, even though God has left the root of faith, Christians, in North Korea. Because they only think of survival their eyes and their ears are closed.

Findings

According to Candice, God has never abandoned North Korea, but has continued to provide for and spiritually minister to the North Koreans. Contrasting other participants, Candice felt that God allowed the famine to happen in North Korea, similar to the time the Israelites spent wandering the desert.

Later in the interview, Candice again compared North Koreans to the Israelites in the desert. Candice was reflecting on the sins of the leaders, and I asked a clarifying question if she was referring to the government or Kim regime. Candice replied:

> It's the government too. Because they don't call on God. They close their ears. Whenever I think of North Koreans, it makes me think of the Israelites. Because when Moses climbed up Mount Sinai, the leaders of Israel at that time wanted to create idols, a gold calf. It's quite similar to the situation in North Korea. Because people in North Korea they just worship the idols of humans, even though now people in North Korea didn't experience the grace of God, but when it comes to worshipping idols, that's why I think of Israel.

Candice was very clear, however, that she did not believe that God was punishing North Koreans. From her perspective, the sins that God should punish belong to the leaders, not to the general populace, who are the victims of the leaders. Candice had this to say regarding God's judgment:

> However, what I believe is that God punishes [if] ancestors' sin to the third and fourth generation. . . . But the people in North Korea have been punished by Kim's family and sins as they are living there. So, the people of North Korea are innocent; it's unfair for them.

Candice then summarized her thoughts on God's punishment by saying, "Being punished by God is right if people made sin, but the person who should be punished by God is Kim's family."

Both Chloe and Miracle spoke of the Israelites in exile in Babylon as an explanation for the situation of North Korea. Chloe used the analogy as her own explanation, comparing the famine in North Korea to Israel in exile, saying:

> Like in the Bible, Israel was arrested by Babylon for seventy years. They were slaves. During the seventy years, that period was the chance of showing God to them. So, it was the same for the North Koreans.

Evil: A North Korean Christian Refugee Perspective

However, Chloe did not equate the famine with punishment for sin. In fact, according to Chloe, there are more sinners in South Korea. Chloe explained her thoughts:

> But there are more sinners in South Korean than North Korea, for example, in homosexuality. South Koreans have freedom to do everything; it lets them make more sins in terms of Jesus. Even though North Koreans are struggling under the government and they experienced the famine, it was God's work to show himself to North Koreans. Some North Koreans who believed in God in China went back to North Korea and are still living there.

Ultimately, Chloe understood the famine as part of God's work to rescue North Koreans, not as punishment, saying, "During the famine North Koreans could escape North Korea. And among them, some people came to believe in God. So, the period of famine was the chance to believe in God."

Miracle used the same analogy of the Israelites in exile, but it was an analogy that she had heard in South Korea, and one which she disagreed with. Miracle explained what pastors had told her, saying, "Oh, all the time pastors compare North Korea to Israel. So, God led Israel [from Babylon] after seventy years.... They were servants for seventy years. During that time, pastors compare Israel during that period with the North Korean situation."

While this analogy is familiar to Miracle, she did not think it was accurate for the North Korean situation. Miracle characterized the North Korean practice of bowing to the statues as "idol worship," but she differentiated that from the idol worship that Israel was punished for, because unlike Israel, North Koreans had not rejected a God they knew. Miracle explained:

> What I think is that, during that time Israel knew God, but they chose other idols. So, it can be sin. But in the case of North Korea, they don't know about God. And it wasn't their choice to choose Kim Il Sung and Kim Jong Il. It's their fault, the government's fault, the Kim family's fault and sin. So, I don't think it's fair.

Miracle did not think it would be fair to judge the people for the sins of the Kim regime.

Jane, on the other hand, had the conviction that everything that happens is part of God's plan, including the suffering in North Korea. I asked Jane if she felt that God was punishing North Korea and she replied, "I think so. Just partly, not totally, but partly. Because in God's sight, I don't know His sight, maybe he loves people, His people." This was again linked to the idea of God "forcing" the North Korean government to destroy itself. Jane stated that the North Korean government is "selling their resources now. But it's a very valuable thing. But they sell cheaply and that means that they just destroy themselves. And I mean everything works just through God." Jane was the only participant to suggest that God was in fact partially punishing North Korea.

SUMMARY

In this chapter, I have presented the study findings which demonstrate that North Korean Christians described evil as oppression of the vulnerable. Oppression of the vulnerable is expressed in the participants' descriptions of government actions. Participants described the evil of government actions in general, and with specific examples about the lack of human rights in North Korea, the evil of public executions carried out in North Korea, and rampant poverty throughout the country. These findings demonstrated that participants described evil as a power dynamic where those in power oppress the vulnerable.

Participants described evil as predominately caused by people and institutions. Participants described evil and the fallenness of humankind through examples of human trafficking, sexual violations, and discrimination. Participants shared examples of how the North Korean government oppresses its people, the Chinese government and human traffickers oppresses North Korean refugees, and men sexually oppress women. Additionally, they shared how North Korean refugees were discriminated against by South Koreans, the Chinese, and other North Korean refugees. These findings demonstrate that participants described evil as a power dynamic where those in power oppress the vulnerable.

Finally, participants understand and describe the sovereignty of God in terms of God's plan and timing for both individuals and for both North and South Korea. Participants also discussed some questions and doubts they have about God's plan, with some participants sharing about how they have resolved their questions and some sharing about how their questions remain unanswered. Furthermore, the findings demonstrate that participants understand and describe God as just and caring about North Koreans. Participants expressed their understanding of the justice of God as God not abandoning or punishing North Koreans, but working to rescue the North Korean people in the future.

6

Discussion

THE PURPOSE OF THIS basic qualitative study was to understand how North Korean Christian refugees describe evil based on their lived experiences. In the findings chapter I presented data which demonstrated that participants understand and describe evil as the oppression of the vulnerable, a power dynamic in which those in power dominate the vulnerable. For my participants, the powerful who oppress the vulnerable were primarily described as humans and human institutions, including specific references to government actions. Other examples of evil that participants described included how human traffickers oppress North Korean refugees, how men sexually oppress women, and how North Korean refugees are discriminated against by South Koreans, the Chinese, and other North Korean refugees. Participants expressed a belief in the sovereignty of God and a trust in God's plan, while simultaneously expressing some doubts, both lingering and resolved, about God's plan. Participants also discussed an understanding of God as someone who is both good and just, and who will rescue the North Korean people from oppression.

In this chapter I will discuss the findings in light of existing academic literature. The chapter is organized into four main sections; in each section, I discuss a major finding. I have organized the chapter in light of this study's research questions. In the first part, I discuss the findings related to the central research question: How do North Korean Christian refugees understand and describe evil based on their lived experiences? This first section includes a discussion of the findings in light of the sub-questions about how participants describe the causes of evil and the fallenness of humankind in

Discussion

light of evil. Next, I will discuss the findings in regards to the sub-question concerning how participants understand and describe the sovereignty of God in light of evil. Finally, I will discuss the findings in connection with the final sub-question concerning how participants understand and describe the goodness of God in light of evil.

EVIL AS THE OPPRESSION OF THE VULNERABLE

One of the major findings of this study was that evil was described as the oppression of the vulnerable. Participants described the vulnerable as the common people in North Korea, North Korean refugees in China and in South Korea, and women. Conversely, the participants described oppressors as the North Korean government and elites, human traffickers, and men. For participants, evil was present in government oppression, sexual assault, human trafficking, and discrimination. The findings showed that the actions of the powerful, which includes actors such as the North Korean government, the Chinese government, human traffickers, and men, over the vulnerable, is an inseparable part of the nature of evil. The findings intersect with the literature of the North Korean lived experience, specifically that participants experienced many phenomena common to the North Korean refugee experience, and described those experiences as evil.[1]

In this section, I will first discuss the major finding of evil as the oppression of the vulnerable, especially acts committed by the North Korean government. This will include a discussion on the ideology of *Juche* and how the findings intersect with the literature about *Juche*.[2] Next, I will discuss the oppression of the vulnerable through the experience of refugees. The findings demonstrated that participants understand the cause of evil to be human actions, as I will show in the sections on government oppression and the refugee experience. However, a minor finding also highlighted the role of spiritual forces in the experience of evil. I will conclude this section discussing this minor finding as it intersects with the literature on Korean shamanism.

---

1. Kim et al., "Understanding Social Exclusion"; Kim et al., "Pre-migration Trauma"; Transitional Justice Working Group, *Exploring Grassroots*; Transitional Justice Working Group, *Mapping the Fate*, 29–41; Ulferts and Howard, "North Korean Human Rights."

2. See Belke, *Juche*; Myers, *Juche Myth*; Wolman, "South Korea's Response."

Evil: A North Korean Christian Refugee Perspective

Governmental Oppression of the Vulnerable

The findings included descriptions of evil as the North Korean government, which oppresses the vulnerable populace. My participants talked specifically about the lack of human rights in North Korea when talking about evil. They also shared about public executions and the rampant poverty throughout the country. My findings align with the literature that has already established that the North Korean refugee experience is filled with trauma and hardship, often due to the North Korean government.[3]

The Transnational Justice Working Group conducted a mixed-methods study with North Koreans in South Korea.[4] They found several trauma-causing events, which included beatings, sexual assault, forced repatriation, detention, and starvation. The Transnational Justice Working Group found that nearly 75 percent of participants experienced these traumatic events.[5] Additionally, their study indicated that participants held the North Korean regime as responsible for the acts of trauma. Furthermore, 85 percent of the participants identified themselves as victims of the North Korean government.[6]

The findings from my study align with the Transnational Justice Working Group regarding the types of traumatic events. My findings included the types of traumatic events listed by the Transnational Justice Working Group.[7] For example, my participants held the North Korean regime as responsible for the evil and suffering of the North Korean people. Furthermore, the findings also demonstrated that North Korean refugees identify with victims who experience trauma at the hands of the North Korean government, with some of my participants self-identifying as victims themselves.

My findings included one aspect of trauma that is not adequately discussed in the literature: the trauma of public executions. While the literature mentions executions or public executions, it only briefly discussed how the trauma of witnessing a public execution impacts North Koreans:

---

3. Kim et al., "Understanding Social Exclusion"; Kim et al., "Pre-migration Trauma"; Transitional Justice Working Group, *Exploring Grassroots*; Transitional Justice Working Group, *Mapping the Fate*; Ulferts and Howard, "North Korean Human Rights," 86.
4. Transitional Justice Working Group, *Exploring Grassroots*, 14–15.
5. Transitional Justice Working Group, *Exploring Grassroots*, 23.
6. Transitional Justice Working Group, *Exploring Grassroots*, 25.
7. Transitional Justice Working Group, *Exploring Grassroots*, 23.

> The consequences of state-sanctioned killings for the family members of those killed can extend well beyond the incident itself and the personal loss involved. At the individual level, for example, according to our research, the psychological effects of witnessing a public execution could include nightmares, insomnia, and loss of appetite after the event. At the community level, the psychological and socio-cultural impact is deliberately designed to consolidate the regime's control over the behavior of citizens.[8]

My participants who had witnessed a public execution while in North Korea were tremendously impacted by the experience, considered it to be a traumatic event, and described it as a prime example of evil. Similar to what the Transnational Justice Working Group found,[9] my findings included discussions of nightmares and the loss of appetite from witnessing public executions. Moreover, the findings demonstrated how the lives of the participants continue to be negatively impacted by witnessing public executions.

My findings also indicated participants understood the forced observations of public executions to be attempts at behavior control, which is in line with the research conducted by the Transnational Justice Working Group.[10] The trauma of public executions is described by participants as evil events used to instill both fear of the government as well as hatred for those who are disloyal to the government. One reason that the literature is limited in discussing the lasting trauma of experiencing a public execution may be due to North Koreans being reticent to discuss the experience. For example, one of my participants who experienced a public execution chose not to discuss it, yet freely discussed other traumatic events.

My study also produced findings that align with the literature on pre-migration trauma in the area of human rights violations and lack of basic freedoms. In their work, Ulferts and Howard mentioned starvation, political prisons, and the lack of basic freedoms such as freedom of movement and freedom of speech, as components in the North Korean context.[11] In regards to starvation, Ulferts and Howard held the North Korean government responsible for the famine during the 1990s.[12]

---

8. Transitional Justice Working Group, *Mapping the Fate*, 51.
9. Transitional Justice Working Group, *Mapping the Fate*, 51.
10. Transitional Justice Working Group, *Mapping the Fate*, 51.
11. Ulferts and Howard, "North Korean Human Rights," 85–86.
12. Ulferts and Howard, "North Korean Human Rights," 86.

Evil: A North Korean Christian Refugee Perspective

My findings showed that participants shared these experiences directly or indirectly, and found them to be both traumatic and evil. The findings showed that both political prisons and lack of freedoms were mentioned specifically as the worst actions of the North Korean government. My findings also supported the assertion of Ulferts and Howard that the North Korean government was responsible for starvation in North Korea,[13] as participants who had experienced famine blamed it on the North Korean government as well.

In all the experiences of pre-migration trauma, participants ultimately held the North Korean government as responsible. My findings suggested that participants believe that the government and its leaders, which assert dominance over every aspect of life, must also bear responsibility for the experience of evil and suffering in the country, even if the evil act that was committed was done by a low ranking official.

JUCHE

In chapter 2 I reviewed literature concerning *Juche* because I anticipated that it would emerge in my findings. While participants did not explicitly talk about *Juche*, the ideology is still relevant to my study. In particular, *Juche* ideology is a part of the government oppression of the vulnerable. My participants' worldview differs from what is postulated by *Juche*, particularly in what is evil and concerning the notion of human agency. In this section, I will first discuss the findings and literature around the role of *Juche* in North Korea, placing my research alongside authors who posited that *Juche* plays a significant role in the daily life of North Koreans.[14] I will then discuss how my participants differ from the *Juche* worldview, and in fact, invert it. Specifically, participants reject the *Juche* postulation that the North Korean people are masters of their own destiny, but rather blame the government for their experience of evil.

ROLE OF JUCHE

The literature surrounding the role *Juche* had two different streams of thought; first, that *Juche* played an integral role in the life of North Koreans,[15]

---

13. Ulferts and Howard, "North Korean Human Rights," 86.
14. Belke, *Juche*, 1–3; Cho, "Encounter," 96–97; Kang, "Lens of *Juche*," 45.
15. See Belke, *Juche*; Kang, "Lens of *Juche*."

or that *Juche* is merely a smokescreen to hide North Korea's true ideology of militant ethno-nationalism.[16] My findings indicated that the participants' experience of daily life was filled with expressions of *Juche* as found in the literature. For example, participants understood the frequent bowing before the pictures and idols of Kim Il Sung and Kim Jong Il as worship, as suggested by Belke.[17] This is further reiterated in the findings where, after their conversion to Christianity, participants considered their previous acts of prostration and veneration to be sinful acts from which they needed to repent. The findings also referred to the Kim regime as setting themselves up as gods to be worshipped, as mentioned by Belke.[18]

The findings demonstrated that participants do not agree with Myers' assertions that *Juche* is designed to mask the real ruling ideology of North Korea.[19] The findings paint a picture where, far from a smokescreen for international use, participants expressed the tenets of *Juche* as part of daily life. Admittedly, Myers wrote from an international relations lens, and so may be looking at how *Juche* does or does not impact foreign policy. However, the findings suggested that participants understood *Juche* as the ruling ideology, and that *Juche* and the North Korean government could be considered synonymous.

Inverted *Juche*

The findings indicated that participants rejected *Juche* in two main areas: agency and evil. The central point of *Juche* is that humans are masters of the world, or in the words of Kim, "Our leader created the great *Juche* idea after acquiring a deep insight into the requirements of a new era when the oppressed and humiliated masses of the people became masters of their own destiny."[20] My findings, however, demonstrated that participants do not believe that the oppressed masses are masters of their own destiny, but are rather victims who suffer from the evil actions of the *Juche*-led government. Participants blame the government for the oppression of the vulnerable, which is the opposite of what *Juche* posits. Participants overwhelmingly expressed a lack of mastery or agency in their lives when in North Korea.

16. Myers, *Juche Myth*, 3.
17. Belke, *Juche*, 84–85.
18. Belke, *Juche*, 83–84.
19. Myers, *Juche Myth*, 3.
20. Kim, *On the Juche Idea*, 4.

Evil: A North Korean Christian Refugee Perspective

Participants believed that this oppression is normative for the people in North Korea, except for the elites of society. Instead of the oppressed and humiliated masses becoming masters, the findings indicated that the North Korean people traded one form of oppression, the Japanese occupation, for another, the *Juche* state. The very act of fleeing North Korea, which itself is a crime in the *Juche* nation, is an expression of a desire and assumed risk to have some mastery of one's own destiny.

As stated in the literature, evil in the *Juche* worldview is understood as disloyalty to the *Juche* system and disloyalty to the Korean race.[21] My findings demonstrated that disloyalty to the *Juche* system and government is indeed considered evil in the North Korean context. However, my findings also indicated that participants reject this understanding of evil, and believe the *Juche* government system is evil. Furthermore, participants have inverted *Juche*, and hold the government responsible for their situation; disloyalty to the government is an action that they all undertook for their well-being. Where *Juche* asserts that humans are their own masters and create their own good, participants described a North Korean context where the people have very little agency, and suffer from the actions of the government.

EVIL AND THE FALLENNESS OF HUMANKIND: REFUGEE EXPERIENCES

The findings in my study demonstrated that participants understood evil as intertwined with the fallenness of humankind. Evil is both caused by human actions and experienced by human beings. The findings highlighted three main areas that typified evil and the fallenness of humankind. These three areas were the experiences of: human trafficking, sexual violations, and discrimination. These areas are inexorably connected with participants' experience as refugees, as all these experiences took place in the context of migration or resettlement.

In the following section, I will discuss the findings in connection with the refugee experience. Specifically, I will discuss the literature and findings surrounding migration trauma, gender-based violence, and adjustment difficulties and discrimination. Finally, I will discuss the minor finding of spiritual agency in evil with the literature found in chapter 2.

---

21. Belke, *Juche*, 13–17; Myers, *Cleanest Race*, 8–11.

Migration Trauma

The findings are overwhelmingly in agreement with the previous literature written on the migration hardships of refugees in general,[22] and with North Korean refugees specifically.[23] The findings in my study demonstrated an experience of trauma at repatriation events. My participants all expressed fear and hatred of the repatriation policies of China. In their quantitative study examining post-traumatic stress disorder (PTSD) amongst North Korean refugees, Kim et al. found that North Korean refugees who personally experienced repatriation were more likely to suffer from PTSD. However, only 20 percent of North Korean refugees surveyed experienced a repatriation event.[24] My findings are in alignment with Kim et al. in that, while repatriation events are present and traumatic, it is personally experienced by a minority of participants.[25] Presumably this is because individuals who are repatriated are imprisoned and sometimes executed; thus, participants who escape are less likely to have experienced repatriation.

Gender-Based Violence against Women

My findings also demonstrated gender-based violence during migration. Several participants used the examples of sexual assault and oppression of North Korean women by Chinese men to epitomize evil. The findings did not limit the sexual violations to only Chinese men, however, as fellow North Korean refugees were also identified as perpetrators of sexual violence. It should be noted that the perpetrators of sexual violence in this study were all men; there was nothing in the findings that suggested any type of sexual assault committed by a woman. In the findings, the experiences of sexual violence were all characterized by male perpetrators and female victims.

The findings also supported the experience of gendered-based violence during migration by the fact that none of the male participants mentioned experiencing or witnessing any violence during their own journeys. The male participants did express experiencing hardships, such

---

22. Gebreyesus et al., "Violence en Route," 721–43; Willams et al., "Child Protection and Sexual Exploitation," 158–66.

23. See Chun, "Representation and Self-Presentation"; Emery et al., "After the Escape"; Kim et al., "Understanding Social Exclusion"; Kim et al., "Pre-migration Trauma"; Lee, "Educational Experiences"; Poorman, "North Korean Defectors";

24. Kim et al., "Pre-migration Trauma," 468–69.

25. Kim et al., "Pre-migration Trauma," 468–69.

Evil: A North Korean Christian Refugee Perspective

as hunger or hiding from the Chinese police, but no violent experiences were shared. As in the overarching findings of this study, the vulnerable, in this case women refugees, experienced evil and suffering at the hands of the powerful, in this case men.

Prior studies have examined or highlighted gender-based or sexual violence that refugees can experience.[26] Kim et al. found that among North Korean refugees, women were more likely to suffer from PTSD than men, indicating a gendered component in traumatic events.[27] Emery et al. found that 63 percent of female participants experienced PTSD, with nearly 20 percent of victims experiencing sexual violence at the hands of North Korean authorities.[28] In my findings, however, there was not discussion around sexual violence at the hands of the North Korean government. Rather, according to my findings, sexual violence was associated with Chinese men and other North Korean refugees.

Williams et al. found that poverty and vulnerability led to refugee women suffering sexual exploitation.[29] In particular, the lack of food or money coupled with the ability to earn money from sex work led women to suffer sexual exploitation.[30] However, in my findings, while poverty was linked with the sexual exploitation of women, it was the risk of repatriation that highlighted the vulnerability of women to suffer sexual exploitation and violence. North Korean refugees have no rights in China, and are extremely vulnerable to repatriation. Additionally, my findings demonstrated that participants were economically vulnerable as well, leading to an increased risk of sexual exploitation.

The study conducted by Gebreyesus et al. highlighted isolated terrain, dependence on human smugglers, and the risk of trafficking as factors that increased the vulnerability of sexual violence among women refugees during migration.[31] My findings demonstrated that those specific three factors were all part of the experience of North Korean refugees during migration. In other words, the very context that Gebreyesus et al. highlighted

---

26. See Emery et al., "After the Escape"; Gebreyesus et al., "Violence en Route," 721–43; Kim et al., "Pre-migration Trauma," 471; Willams et al., "Child Protection and Sexual Exploitation," 158–66.

27. Kim et al., "Pre-migration Trauma," 471.

28. Emery et al., "After the Escape," 1010.

29. Willams et al., "Child Protection and Sexual Exploitation," 161–64.

30. Willams et al., "Child Protection and Sexual Exploitation," 162.

31. Gebreyesus et al., "Violence en Route," 738.

Discussion

as factors for increased vulnerability of sexual violence[32] is the context through which North Korean refugees must flee.

My findings also showed a normalization, or at the very least an expectation, of sexual violence during migration. Additionally, data included stories about a type of systemization of sexual violence in the forced sale of women refugees into the sex industry in China. This aligns somewhat with Gebreyesus et al. findings that sexual violence was normalized and systematized during the migration of women.[33]

The findings in my study add to the ongoing academic conversation in the literature surrounding sexual violence and women refugees. The North Korean women who escaped through China risk sexual exploitation and violence from brokers, Chinese men, and other refugees. Poverty and lack of legal rights in China further increased this risk.

Discrimination and Adjustment Difficulties

My findings demonstrated participants described evil as the discrimination they had experienced along with the difficulties they had in adjusting to life in South Korea. The experiences of discrimination included feeling "othered" for having a North Korean accent, experiencing physical confrontations, and suffering an online form of abuse. One participant even shared about a North Korean refugee who resettled in the USA to escape the discrimination in South Korea. Scholars have highlighted several ways that North Korean refugees experience adjustment difficulties and discrimination in South Korea, including lack of education,[34] social capital, a stigma against North Koreans,[35] and not settling in South Korea to avoid ongoing discrimination.[36]

My study also demonstrated that participants were generally successful in their education and studies. While this does not indicate that participants were free from struggle in their studies, it does indicate that the participants demonstrated success in overcoming the educational disadvantage they face. Yeom and Ward's study found that North Korean

---

32. Gebreyesus et al., "Violence en Route," 738.
33. Gebreyesus et al., "Violence en Route," 738.
34. Yeom and Ward, "Integrating North Korean Refugee," 29–39.
35. Hamad, "Language Split," 24–25; Han et al., "Depression in North Korean Refugees," 283–89.
36. Kim and Atteraya, "North Korean Refugees' Intention," 1197.

refugees struggle in the South Korean education system.[37] However, participants in my study had a high graduation rate, without any participant reporting that they dropped out of the education system. This may be because several of the organizations that helped connect me to my initial participants are organizations that support North Korean refugees in university in South Korea.

In their mixed-methods study, Han et al. found high levels of depression among North Korean refugees in South Korea.[38] Han et al. found that some contributing factors for the high levels of depression included maladjustment to South Korean society, past trauma, and loneliness.[39] However, my findings did not demonstrate high levels of depression amongst North Korean refugees in South Korea, even though the findings do support the experience of maladjustment to South Korean society, past trauma, and loneliness. Admittedly, my study was not focused on these issues and so I did not ask questions regarding depression or overall mental health; still, the only mention of depression or feeling depressed was by a participant who referred to life in North Korea, not South Korea.

Notably, participants described their experiences of discrimination as evil. North Korean refugees are granted legal citizenship in South Korea.[40] However, there is a power dynamic at play, in which South Koreans have educational, financial, social, and linguistic advantages over North Koreans. The findings show that participants experienced educational, financial, social, and linguistic deficits, which contributed to a difficulty in adjusting to South Korean society.

Evil Caused by Spiritual Actions

While the findings predominantly found human actions to be responsible for evil, participants also described spiritual activity as a cause of evil. Both Eckert et al.[41] and Grayson[42] discussed Korean shamanism's belief that spirits are regional beings with different characteristics in different areas, while the shamanistic understanding of spirits spreading disease

---

37. Yeom and Ward, "Integrating North Korean Refugee," 37.
38. Han et al., "Depression in North Korean Refugees," 285.
39. Han et al., "Depression in North Korean Refugees," 286.
40. Kim and Atteraya, "North Korean Refugees' Intention," 1189.
41. Eckert et al., *Korea Old and New*, 50.
42. Grayson, *Korea*, 221–25.

was discussed by Bruno,[43] Hogarth,[44] and Walraven.[45] According to Eckert et al., Korean shamanistic beliefs hold spirits responsible for natural disasters in certain areas.[46]

In his anthropological study, Hogarth used the concept of reciprocity as developed by Mauss to examine shamanistic rituals in South Korea.[47] Hogarth described Korean shamanism as a reciprocal relationship between humans and local spirits; sickness and evil befall people when spirits are upset, and thus rituals are needed to appease them.[48]

My findings demonstrated that some participants discussed spiritual activity in that they mentioned regional spirits and spreading disease, particularly COVID-19. This aligns with the literature on the beliefs of Korean shamanism.[49] However, my findings diverge with the literature about Korean shamanism concerning the notion that spirits need to be appeased, as Hogarth asserted.[50] Rather, my findings show that spiritual activity, which was termed demonic, is perceived to be actions that are meant to keep people from coming to faith in God.

While participants could have emphasized spiritual forces in their description of evil, the findings overwhelmingly demonstrate that participants hold humans, and not spirits, responsible for evil. The fallenness of humankind was understood by participants in terms of what they experienced as refugees: migration trauma, gender-based violence against women, and discrimination. The fear of repatriation during migration was especially traumatic, which was also utilized by men to commit sexual violations against women.

EVIL AND THE SOVEREIGNTY OF GOD: THEOLOGICAL BELIEFS

My study highlighted that North Korean Christian refugees' ideas about evil, justice, goodness, and sovereignty were based on their religious

43. Bruno, "Shamanic Ritual," 340.
44. Hogarth, "Pursuit of Happiness," 49.
45. Walraven, "Creation of the World," 246.
46. Eckert et al., *Korea Old and New*, 22.
47. See Hogarth, "Pursuit of Happiness"; Mauss, *Gift*.
48. Hogarth, "Pursuit of Happiness," 59.
49. Bruno, "Shamanic Ritual," 340; Hogarth, "Pursuit of Happiness," 49; Walraven, "Creation of the World," 244–49.
50. Hogarth, "Pursuit of Happiness," 59.

Evil: A North Korean Christian Refugee Perspective

beliefs. However, individuals do not always maintain internal consistency between what they profess to believe as part of a faith and what they actually believe.[51] Discussing the findings using theodicy as a focal point enables the findings on evil, sovereignty, and goodness to connect with the religious literature, as theodicy is an attempt to reconcile an omnipotent and good God with the experience of suffering in the world.[52] Additionally, all participants expressed a belief in a loving, omnipotent, and good God in light of evil existing, which is the basis for Mackie's postulation of the problem of evil that theodicy attempts to reconcile.[53]

In this section, I will discuss the findings in relation to the literature on the Christian beliefs of the sovereignty of God and theodicy. I will first discuss the historical Korean Christian views on evil and God's sovereignty.[54] Next, I will discuss the Calvinist and Arminian understandings of God's sovereignty and evil.[55]

The literature on the historical Korean Christian view of the sovereignty of God in light of the experience of evil highlighted three approaches that Korean Christians have expressed to address the question of theodicy: the teleological understanding as expressed by Augustine Chong Yak-Chong;[56] the divine punishment understanding as expressed by Alexander Sayong Hwang,[57] and the personalized character approach as expressed by Thomas An Chunggun.[58] The findings demonstrated a connection with each of these views, with participants resonating with the teleological and personalized understandings of evil, and rejecting the divine punishment understanding.

---

51. Samples, *World of Difference*.
52. Hall et al., "Theodicy or Not?," 263.
53. Mackie, *Evil*, 200–201.
54. Baker and Rausch, *Catholics in Korea*, 151–203; Rausch, "Suffering History," 69–97.
55. See Alcorn, *If God Is Good*; Boyd, *Satan and the Problem of Evil*; Hale-Smith et al., "Measuring Beliefs," 856; Wilt et al., "God's Role," 352–62.
56. Rausch, "Suffering History," 72.
57. Baker and Rausch, *Catholics in Korea*, 195.
58. Rausch, "Suffering History," 79.

Teleological Understanding of Evil

The teleological understanding of evil is the term I am using to describe the ideas concerning theodicy put forth by Augustine Chong Yak-Chong,[59] and, more recently, Wright.[60] Augustine Chong Yak-Chong taught that ultimate reckoning will not take place until after death,[61] while Wright similarly suggested that while humans cannot understand evil now, people can trust that God's justice will be done to evil in the end. For both Augustine Chong Yak-Chong and Wright, it is only in the light of the telos, the end, that evil can be understood. There is a deep trust in the ultimate goodness of God that will make sense of evil, and that in the end, all things will be well.

The findings showed that participants connected with the teleological understanding of evil. The findings demonstrated a similar teleological trust in God; while participants long for liberation and justice to come to North Korea now, they know that it will take place in the life to come. For participants, the evil and suffering in North Korea cannot and will not make sense in this lifetime; only in the light of eternity will they understand.

Augustine Chong Yak-Chong also wrote about the limits of earthly justice: "Earthly rewards and punishments cannot completely satisfy justice—a murderer who has killed many people can only be killed once."[62] The findings demonstrated a similar belief in some participants, who acknowledged that earthly justice done to the North Korean government would be insufficient, necessitating eternal judgment, specifically mentioning hell.

Another component to the teleological understanding of evil is that it does not necessarily look for or assume a greater purpose for evil and suffering. Thus, while Alcorn argued that one reason God permits personal or natural disasters is so that humans can witness great acts of heroism,[63] Wright responded to that assertion by saying, "Various writers have suggested, for instance, that God allows evil because it creates the special conditions in which virtue can flourish. But the thought that God decided to permit Auschwitz because some heroes would emerge is hardly a solution to the problem."[64]

59. Rausch, "Suffering History," 72.
60. Wright, *Evil and the Justice of God*, 137–43.
61. Rausch, "Suffering History," 72.
62. Rausch, "Suffering History," 72.
63. Alcorn, *If God Is Good*, 392–93, 420.
64. Wright, *Evil and the Justice of God*, 28.

Evil: A North Korean Christian Refugee Perspective

While the findings demonstrated that participants do trust that God is in control and has a plan, the findings did not show that participants held any belief that God is permitting evil and suffering so that virtue can flourish. On the contrary, the findings demonstrated that evil and suffering are caused by the sinful actions of the powerful to the detriment of innocent vulnerable people, without an understood design for heroism or virtue.

Bradshaw and Fitchett, when discussing what I have termed the teleological understanding of evil, characterized this belief of someday things will make sense as "delaying the theodicy question."[65] In their understanding, trusting in the eventual explanation and justice from God was delaying the wrestling match with the theodicy question.[66]

However, the findings demonstrated that, rather than delaying the theodicy question, some participants fully engaged with the theodicy question, and resolved, not delayed, the question teleologically. These participants did not shy away from the vastness of the theodicy question, but rather, facing it head on, came to terms with the fact that they will not be able to answer this question and resolved to trust that God is good, and that his justice will prevail.

The teleological understanding of evil is linked with a solid belief in the goodness of God. The findings demonstrated that participants did not question the goodness of God, but placed their hope in the ultimate plan that God would work out eventually, which would be good. The findings and the goodness of God will be further discussed in a section below.

Divine Determination of Evil

The divine determination of evil is the term used by Daugherty et al. to describe the idea that people suffer evil due to God's direct action,[67] as purported by Alexander Sayong Hwang. Alexander Sayong Hwang, in his famous silk letter, placed the blame of the Korean people on their own sin, stating, "Because we are sinners filled with heavy sin and wickedness, spiritually, we have become the targets of the Lord's anger, and due to our lack of wisdom and understanding, we have lost the sympathy of other people."[68] This understanding put forth by Alexander Sayong Hwang echoes what participants in both this current study and the study conducted by Yoo

---

65. Bradshaw and Fitchett, "God, Why?," 180.
66. Bradshaw and Fitchett, "God, Why?," 180.
67. Daugherty et al., "Measuring Theodicy," 43–44.
68. Hwang and Kim, "Silk Letter," 168.

expressed they had been told by pastors in South Korea and in China regarding the suffering of the North Korean people; namely, that God was punishing the North Korean people for their sins.[69]

A similar understanding of evil was suggested by Bradshaw and Fitchett, who found that participants in their study all believed in a simple cause and effect understanding of evil, in which bad things happen to bad people, while good things happen to good people.[70] The participants in Bradshaw and Fitchett's study, while holding this belief, also expressed confusion as to why they would be suffering, as they believed that they were not bad people.[71]

My participants overwhelmingly rejected this understanding. The findings showed that participants disagreed with this notion both logically and theologically. In other words, participants disagreed with the divine punishment view of evil logically, as those who they believe as most deserving of punishment, the North Korean regime, are the best off in North Korea. Furthermore, participants disagreed with the divine punishment view theologically, as participants did not believe it matches with God's character. Additionally, participants found the idea of North Koreans being under God's punishment as both offensive and hurtful. According to the findings, if there was divine punishment that should fall upon North Korea, it should fall upon the government.

Closely related to the idea of divine punishment and cause and effect is the great law of returns postulated by Plantinga, in which Plantinga explains evil using the proverb "you reap what you sow."[72] And while Plantinga generalized the great law of returns as normative, he did admit that this is not the uniform experience in the world. Plantinga says, "For example, although good and bad parents tend to reproduce in kind, they sometimes raise surprises. Some rotten parents produce good children; some terrific parents produce awful children."[73]

The findings demonstrated that, in the case of the North Korea experience of evil, participants reject the great law of returns, at least on a personal level. The evil that the population has suffered is not due to reaping what they sowed, or reaping what the Christians in Japanese-occupied Korea

69. Yoo, *Learning Experiences*, 280.
70. Bradshaw and Fitchett, "God, Why?," 182.
71. Bradshaw and Fitchett, "God, Why?," 179–86.
72. Plantinga, *Breviary of Sin*, 69.
73. Plantinga, *Breviary of Sin*, 69.

sowed, but rather, reaping what their government has sowed. In another sense, the great law of returns remains true in that the government has sowed poverty and destruction, but it is the common people who reap it. If the great law of returns is normative, the findings show that participants would hold the example of North Korea to be an exception.

Rather than the great law of returns, the findings demonstrated that participants describe evil and suffering in a way that is more in alignment with the chaos understanding of evil, as put forth by Thweatt-Bates. Thweatt-Bates, in discussing the great law of returns as described by Plantinga, stated that Plantinga "fails to consider two things: first, that the consequences of an act are often disproportionate to the act, and second, that consequences are far-reaching, affecting not only the perpetrator of evil but also those innocent of the wrongdoing."[74] The findings demonstrated that participants expressed similar thoughts; that the evil participants had experienced and witnessed were far-reaching, and those affected by evil are often viewed as innocent. My participants' description of evil and suffering was not a linear progression, but a dynamic that gave birth to increasingly more evil, as explained in chaos theory.[75]

Personalized Understanding of Evil

Thomas An Chunggun, who famously assassinated the Japanese Prime Minister Ito Hirobumi, expressed an understanding of evil that placed the blame of the Korean people's suffering at the hands the one man he killed.[76] Thomas An Chunggun personalized evil, and believed that if the leader of the government, Ito Hirobumi, was eliminated, that the suffering of the Korean people would be alleviated.

The findings showed a nuanced connection with this understanding of evil. Some participants would align with the ideology of Thomas An Chunggun, and confessed to wanting to see the leaders of the regime to die, with one participant actually admitting that he would kill the leader himself. Many participants held the leader personally responsible for the evil and suffering of the North Korean people, and in some cases, absolving direct perpetrators of violence from guilt because they believed it was ultimately the fault of Kim Jong Eun.

---

74. Thweatt-Bates, "Chaos and the Problem of Evil," 66.
75. Thweatt-Bates, "Chaos and the Problem of Evil," 65–66.
76. Rausch, "Suffering History," 80.

Discussion

This personalized understanding of evil aligns with the study of Cerci and Colucci, in which victims make a distinction between collaborators and those primarily responsible for evil.[77] In their systematic review of prior studies examining forgiveness and PTSD, Cerci and Colucci found a difference in PTSD symptoms in victims who had forgiven a perpetrator versus those who had forgiven collaborators, as "collaborators were ordered by the principal perpetrator and considered only partially responsible."[78] This would explain why some participants did not harbor bitterness or anger towards the actual individuals that they witnessed committing acts of evil, such as prison guards beating prisoners, as participants understood that those people were just following orders handed down from the government. The findings showed that, in the end, participants understood the principal perpetrator of evil in North Korea to be the government.

However, the findings demonstrated that other participants had a modified version of the personalized understanding of evil, expanding the personal responsibility beyond one person to the entire government system, which in a dictatorship such as North Korea is still directed by one person. What is commonplace throughout the findings, however, is the connection between evil, the North Korean government, and the Kim regime, effectively personalizing evil to the Kim regime.

An example in which participants focused on the personal culpability in evil and not the government is found in the case of sexual violence against women. When discussing sexual violence against women, participants focused on the sin of the perpetrators, and not the actions of a government or institution. The perpetrators use institutional arrangements to exploit and take advantage of vulnerable women, for example, by threatening to turn North Korean women in China into the police to be sent back to North Korea. However, the findings showed that participants hold the perpetrators, and not the institutions, as predominately culpable in the case of sexual violence against women.

Treating sexual violence differently than other forms of experienced trauma aligns with the study conducted by Kandemiri and Nkomo.[79] In their study with Congolese refugees, Kandemiri and Nkomo found that, while participants were able to engage in forgiveness for many traumas

---

77. Cerci and Colucci, "Forgiveness in PTSD," 52.
78. Cerci and Colucci, "Forgiveness in PTSD," 52.
79. Kandemiri and Nkomo, "Congolese Refugees and Asylum Seekers," 551–65.

they experienced during migration, those who experienced sexual violence had a hard time forgiving their perpetrators.[80]

The intimate nature of sexual trauma allows the evil of sexual violence to be personified in the perpetrator, rather than a system. This differs slightly from the findings of Williams et al. which focused on the systemic issues surrounding sexual violence in the Rwandan refugee camps.[81] The findings in my study indicated that in regard to sexual violence, while participants are able to express the systemic issues involved, such as lack of legal rights and a fear of repatriation, they blame the perpetrators of sexual violence, and not the system.

Again, Cerci and Colucci identified the distinction between collaborators and those primarily responsible for evil as a dynamic in which collaborators were ordered to commit acts of evil as part of a system.[82] The findings in this current study did not demonstrate sexual violence to be an ordered action as part of a system, but rather, an intimate violation of men on women. To participants, the perpetrators of sexual violence are intimately culpable for their own evil, regardless of the systemic issues that allow such sexual violence to flourish. Again, the dynamic of the powerful oppressing the vulnerable, in this case, men in China sexually exploiting North Korean women, though personalized, is still the prominent factor expressed by participants.

Calvinist and Arminian Understandings of Evil

The findings in this study showed an interesting convergence in the Calvinist and Arminian understandings of evil and the sovereignty of God; namely that participants adhered to a blueprint theological concept, while at the same time expressing a belief that the evil experienced in North Korea is not a God-ordained event. Prior studies have examined the Calvinist and Arminian understandings of evil,[83] while other authors have discussed the understandings conceptually.[84]

In their research on views of evil and suffering, Hale-Smith et al. considered the Calvinist and Arminian views, referred to as Free Will and Open-Theism respectively, along with the cause and effect view of evil,

80. Kandemiri and Nkomo, "Congolese Refugees and Asylum Seekers," 562.
81. Willams et al., "Child Protection and Sexual Exploitation," 161–64.
82. Cerci and Colucci, "Forgiveness in PTSD," 52.
83. Hale-Smith et al., "Measuring Beliefs," 855–56; Wilt et al., "God's Role," 352–62.
84. Alcorn, *If God Is Good*; Boyd, *Satan and the Problem of Evil*.

referred to as Health and Wealth, to all be mutually exclusive views of evil.[85] Hale-Smith et al. also measured several other beliefs surrounding evil:

> In addition to these mutually exclusive frameworks for suffering, four other beliefs exist that can operate together and with any of the previous beliefs within a theistic framework. The Suffering God perspective emphasizes God's compassionate presence in the midst of suffering.... The Soul-Building perspective emphasizes that God always uses suffering as a challenge.... The Encounter perspective (in both Judaism and Christianity) emphasizes the conversations and complex relationship with God that individuals have in the midst of suffering.... Last, Providence beliefs refer to the level of control over specific events that individuals attribute to God (in this context, control over suffering).[86]

Hale-Smith et al. made the same error that Alcorn made in conflating Open-Theism with the free will defense as postulated by Boyd.[87] By the definitions put forth by Hale-Smith et al., the findings indicate that participants did not line up neatly with the Free Will or Open-Theism understandings of evil, while rejecting the Health and Wealth understanding of evil.

The findings indicated that participants have a mixture of the Calvinist idea of a blueprint theology, or as Hale-Smith et al. termed it, providence, and of the Suffering God perspective.[88] My participants held that God has a plan for North Korea, but His heart is broken regarding the plight of the North Korean people at the hands of the government.

The findings demonstrate that the participants' understanding of providence, as explained by Hale-Smith et al., is complicated. The findings indicated that participants generally do not attribute specific evil events to God, while attributing good events or protection to God. Thus, my participants seem to believe in God's providence in good events, while focusing on God's co-suffering in the midst of evil events, holding in tension the goodness and omnipotence of God with the experience of evil. In this way, the findings resonate with Wilt et al.'s review of the study conducted by Hale-Smith et al., which found, "The limited knowledge scale

---

85. Hale-Smith et al., "Measuring Beliefs," 856.
86. Hale-Smith et al., "Measuring Beliefs," 856.
87. Hale-Smith et al., "Measuring Beliefs," 856.
88. Hale-Smith et al., "Measuring Beliefs," 856.

was positively related to beliefs pertaining to God's benevolence but also positively to beliefs in a random world."[89]

The study by Hale-Smith et al. was designed for a North American sample, and admitted that this study could not be generalized across cultural lines.[90] The findings suggested that, regarding what the instrument developed by Hale-Smith et al. measures, there are aspects of beliefs that are present in North Korean Christian refugees regarding evil. However, it remains to be seen if this specific tool would have validity with a sample outside of North America.

An interesting component of the findings is the way participants both converged and diverged with the Calvinist and Arminian views on causality of evil. The Calvinist view on evil as displayed by Alcorn divided evil into primary evil, which is the moral evil humans commit, and secondary evil, which is the consequences suffered from primary evil.[91] Alcorn described God both as sometimes assigning secondary evil as punishment for people choosing evil, and as having a higher purpose in the evil that people experience.

The findings demonstrated that participants have been previously told a similar explanation of evil, namely that God has assigned the evil in North Korea due to its sin. However, the findings show that participants reject the idea that God has assigned evil. What Alcorn described as secondary evil that is attributable to God, such as suffering, participants attribute to the moral evil of others. The findings demonstrated that participants understand suffering to be the direct result of moral evil caused by those in power, and experienced by the vulnerable. Furthermore, different than Alcorn's suggestion that God assigns people suffering so that they may repent, participants described God as having kindness and love for those who are suffering.[92]

The findings showed a nuanced understanding regarding the notion that God has a higher purpose in the evil that people experience. My study also demonstrated that participants question why God does not intervene in some situations and that some participants expressed a belief that God was working out a plan, while other participants expressed their belief that God is heartbroken over the suffering in North Korea. Thus,

---

89. Wilt et al., "God's Role," 353.
90. Hale-Smith et al., "Measuring Beliefs," 863–64.
91. Alcorn, *If God Is Good*, 26–29.
92. Alcorn, *If God Is Good*, 417.

Discussion

the findings somewhat converged with a type of blueprint theology as described by Boyd and espoused by Alcorn.[93]

Boyd's treatment of the question of why God does not intervene, though rather philosophical, may find resonance with participants who are left asking that question, but continue to express a belief in God's omnipotence.

> It thus does not seem that the explanation for why God tolerates the ongoing destructive activity of rebellious agents is that they mysteriously contribute to a greater good or that they will eventually turn to God. The remaining possibility, I suggest is that God *cannot* immediately terminate their existence. This may initially sound like a denial of God's omnipotence, but it is not. To be sure, if we were to hold that God's inability to immediately terminate evil beings was due to something *extrinsic to God* we would be denying God's omnipotence. But if God's inability is a necessary corollary of decisions he himself has made, then it is the *result* of God's omnipotence, not the denial of it.[94]

The synthesis of holding God as omnipotent while witnessing events that God did not intervene is elaborate, and while no participants used this direct explanation, the findings did demonstrate that some participants thought along similar lines; namely, that God gives freedom and individuals can misuse the freedom, which God allows to happen because freedom is, by definition, free.

The findings also demonstrated that participants do not attribute the secondary evil they have experienced in North Korea to God. Thus, the findings demonstrated that participants converged with the Calvinist idea of a blueprint theology, but diverged with the concept of God assigning secondary evil. While this is may be internally incongruent from a philosophical standpoint, people's worldviews tend to have differing levels of internal congruency.[95]

EVIL AND THE GOODNESS OF GOD

The final sub-question in this research asked how North Korean Christian refugees understood and described the goodness of God in light of evil. The findings demonstrated that participants understood the goodness of

---

93. See Alcorn, *If God Is Good*, 225–37; Boyd, *Satan and the Problem of Evil*.
94. Boyd, *Satan and the Problem of Evil*, 181.
95. Samples, *World of Difference*, 22.

Evil: A North Korean Christian Refugee Perspective

God in a personalized way, which was evident in their search for meaning and understanding in their experiences of evil. Additionally, the findings indicated that participants experienced the goodness of God through the actions of Christians.

Meaning-Making

Meaning-making is an integral part of processing suffering and evil.[96] Viktor Frankl, in his reflection on surviving a concentration camp during the Holocaust, asserted that if a person "knows the 'why' for his existence, he will be able to bear almost any 'how.'"[97] The experience of suffering or trauma is an opportunity for the victim to create situational meaning that aligns with their global worldview.[98] Prior studies have examined meaning-making in light of cancer,[99] suffering in general,[100] and war displacement.[101]

In their qualitative study on how Christians processed cancer diagnoses, Hall et al. utilized a meaning-making model to inform their understanding of suffering, as meaning making seeks to resolve the discrepancies between the global and situational meanings of an experienced event.[102] The study by Hall et al. found that Christian cancer patients did not generally experience tension between their faith and their cancer, with fully two-thirds of the participants not experiencing any tension between the two.[103]

While the participants in Hall et al. generally did not express experiencing tension, my findings demonstrated that participants in this study did express levels of tension and questioning between their faith and their experience of evil. The most animated parts of the interviews in this current study happened when participants expressed the tension they experienced, and wanted to know a reason for the evil they experienced in North Korea. According to the findings, participants in this current study had a conflicted relationship with meaning-making and evil: they both want to know the "why" (a reason for the evil they have witnessed), and they hate any reason they have been given.

> 96. Ahmadi et al., "Meaning-Making," 1794–95.
> 97. Frankl, *Man's Search for Meaning*, 88.
> 98. Hall et al., "Theodicy or Not?," 265.
> 99. Ahmadi et al., "Meaning-Making"; Hall et al., "Theodicy or Not?
> 100. Hall and Hill, "Meaning-Making," 467–71.
> 101. Matos et al., "Syrian Refugees," 3.
> 102. Hall et al., "Theodicy or Not?," 265.
> 103. Hall et al., "Theodicy or Not?," 267.

Additionally, my findings indicated that while participants experienced tensions in their faith, their tensions are resolved through an increased trust and faith in God. In this way, the findings converged with Hall et al., which found that participants tended to experience a deepening of faith through their ordeal, and did not question God's existence amid suffering.[104] Hall et al. stated:

> Rather than questioning God's love, omnipotence, omniscience, or existence, their experience seemed to accentuate their experience of these attributes in the context of the relationship with God. Two themes characterized their responses. The first was an expression of confidence in God, often with an emphasis on God's love and control, or God's personal involvement in the circumstances of their cancer narrative. The second was an expression of spiritual intellectual humility, of not needing to know given God's knowledge and omniscience.[105]

Similar to what Hall et al. described, the findings demonstrated that participants focused on the love of God and his personal closeness to themselves and the North Korean people. Furthermore, the "expression of spiritual intellectual humility"[106] is synonymous with the teleological understanding of evil, which resonated with participants.

In their study on meaning-making, Matos et al. noted that their findings did not contain religious themes, even though their participants were religious.[107] In contrast, my findings demonstrated that meaning making was linked directly to religious beliefs. For participants, meaning making was only discussed using religious language or when discussing God. In particular, my findings showed the meaning making process as asking questions of God and pastors, and through prayer and Bible study.

Goodness of God Experienced through Christians

My findings demonstrated how participants understood the goodness of God in a personalized way. According to my participants, God is for them and for North Korea. The findings indicated that participants began to believe and experience the goodness of God due to the actions of churches and Christians. The findings are aligned with what previous

---

104. Hall et al., "Theodicy or Not?," 268.
105. Hall et al., "Theodicy or Not?," 268–69.
106. Hall et al., "Theodicy or Not?," 269.
107. Matos et al., "Syrian Refugees," 14.

scholars have written about the impact of Christians and churches on North Korean refugees.[108]

Cho found that the majority of North Korean defectors were motivated to become Christians due to the support they received from Christians and churches,[109] while Jun et al.[110] suggested that the relationship between refugees and South Korean Christians was a critical factor in the spiritual growth of refugees.

Lee conducted qualitative research looking at the educational experiences of North Korean refugees while in China.[111] In Lee's study, the findings showed that participants sought help from churches and Christians in China to escape repatriation.[112] Lee's study also found that North Korean refugees were in great fear of being caught or imprisoned in China because of the risk of repatriation.[113]

Nearly all participants in this current study who spent time in China were assisted by Chinese Christians and churches, with some participants being directed there for assistance by non-Christians. This indicates that the literature surrounding the underground church assistance for North Korean refugees is supported by the findings. Furthermore, the findings aligned with the literature in that the churches and missionaries in China assume a great risk in order to help North Korean refugees escape.[114]

SUMMARY OF DISCUSSION

The experience of North Korean refugees has been marked by encounters of evil and suffering, in which the participants experienced the fallenness of humankind. Specifically, evil and the fallenness of humankind are exemplified through the oppression of the vulnerable by those in power. Furthermore, participants rejected and inverted *Juche* ideology, in that participants hold the principal perpetrator, in their case the North Korean government, ultimately responsible for this evil. For my participants, God is responsible for the good they have experienced, and is not directly

---

108. Cho, "Effect of Religion"; Jun et al., "Understanding the Acceptance," 450; Lee, "Educational Experiences," 39.

109. Cho, "Effect of Religion," 256.

110. Jun et al., "Understanding the Acceptance," 450.

111. Lee, "Educational Experiences," 41–43.

112. Lee, "Educational Experiences," 39.

113. Lee, "Educational Experiences," 45–46.

114. Cho, "Effect of Religion," 245; Lee, "Educational Experiences," 47.

Discussion

involved in the evil they have witnessed. Rather, the evil they have experienced is due to evil people in positions of power, whether it be formal authority, gendered power, greater social or linguistic capital, or holding legal leverage over the vulnerable.

Theologically, this research has indicated that participants have a nuanced understanding of evil, that converges and diverges with a variety of aspects of Christian theology, shamanism, and *Juche* ideology. Christianity is the dominant influence on the understanding of evil, with a particular resonance with the teleological and personalized understandings of evil, and a rejection of the divine punishment understanding of evil.

CONTRIBUTIONS, IMPLICATIONS, AND CONCLUSIONS

The purpose of this basic descriptive study was to understand how North Korean Christian refugees understand and describe evil in light of their lived experiences. This research has shown that North Korean Christian refugees understand and describe evil as the oppression of the vulnerable. The findings indicated that the participants identify with the vulnerable, which include North Korean refugees and women. The powerful, according to this research, are primarily seen as humans and human institutions, with special emphasis on the North Korean government. The findings also demonstrated that the participants held traditional orthodox views of the sovereignty of God, while simultaneously expressing some doubts about God's plan due to the experience of evil. This research indicated that the participants reject the idea that God is punishing North Korea, but rather believe that, ultimately, God will one day rescue the North Korean people from oppression. The findings also demonstrated that the participants reject *Juche* ideology, and invert it, whereupon they hold the government as responsible for the evil they have experienced. All in all, this research offers several contributions to theory and implications for practice, which I will discuss next.

Contributions to Theory

This research is significant for the understanding of theodicy, and advances the research that has been conducted regarding the understanding of evil. This research also substantiates earlier research on the North Korean experience, including the experiences of hardship and the role of *Juche* in daily life. Furthermore, this research contributes to the research that has

Evil: A North Korean Christian Refugee Perspective

been conducted concerning refugees. In this next section, I will discuss the contributions to research on theodicy, the North Korean experience, refugees, and *Juche*.

Theodicy

Findings from this research substantiate the assertions of Yoo that evil and suffering are important topics to address with North Korean refugees.[115] This current research has demonstrated that the participants are reflective and eager to understand their experience of evil in light of their faith in an omnipotent and loving God. This research also provides clarity that some theories of theodicy are more acceptable to North Korean refugees than others.

My research has highlighted the importance of teleology in the discussion of theodicy and the problem of evil. While not described as such, the teleological understanding of evil has support in prior Christian scholarship.[116] Additionally, my research demonstrated that the teleological understanding of evil finds resonance with North Korean refugees who are reflecting on their experience of evil and suffering.

My research has demonstrated that previous empirical studies designed to understand evil can be useful in the North Korean context. The categories of sovereignty and causality used in prior studies of evil and theodicy that were conducted with participants in the United States were useful in conceptualizing the North Korean Christian refugee ideas surrounding theodicy.[117] Additionally, this research illuminated that historical Korean Christian understandings of evil and theodicy remain relevant and applicable to current Korean Christian understandings of evil and theodicy. The personified, divine punishment, and teleological understandings of evil are all found in early Korean Christian writings.[118] However, further research should be conducted to understand the process of how North Korean refugees construct their understanding of evil and theodicy. Additionally, further research should be conducted to understand the role that denominational affiliation may play in the construction of theodicy beliefs of North Korean refugees.

115. Yoo, *Learning Experiences*, 279.
116. Hall et al., "Theodicy or Not?"; Rausch, "Suffering History"; Wright, *Evil and the Justice of God*.
117. Hale-Smith et al., "Measuring Beliefs," 856; Wilt et al., "God's Role," 352–62.
118. Rausch, "Suffering History," 71–80.

Discussion

North Korean Experience

This research has corroborated with much of the previous research on the experience of North Koreans, both in the suffering experienced in North Korea, and the vulnerability and discrimination North Korean refugees face in China and South Korea. The findings substantiate previous studies on the prevalence of traumatic events in the lives of North Koreans, including imprisonment, forced relocation, public executions, and human trafficking. The findings also substantiate and further magnify research on the vulnerability that North Koreans refugees face during their escape journey. Specifically, the threat of repatriation to North Korea was highlighted as a significant fear among the North Korean refugees. This current research also furthers the discussion on the experience of discrimination and "othering" that North Korean refugees in South Korea face. In particular, my research demonstrated that North Korean refugees in South Korea are identified through their accent and then face discrimination, leading some North Koreans to change their patterns of speech to avoid identification and "othering."

Refugees

The findings from this study have substantiated previous research on the experience of refugees in general, particularly in migration trauma, the risk of human trafficking, and gender-based violence. This research has corroborated previous studies on the prevalence of PTSD among refugees, as well as the trauma of repatriation. Additionally, this research has corroborated prior studies on the risk that human trafficking poses to refugees during displacement. This study has also added to the literature concerning the vulnerability of women to sexual violence during migration. Specifically, my research supports previous studies on factors that put women refugees at risk for sexual violence. These factors include lack of legal rights, a reliance on brokers or human traffickers, and traveling through remote and isolated terrain.

My research also furthers the discussion on the importance of legal rights for refugees, specifically in China. The findings from my study highlighted the fear, trauma, and impact of the Chinese repatriation policy on North Korean refugees. The findings showed that the threat of repatriation was particularly used by perpetrators to commit gender-based violence against North Korean women who are refugees in China.

Evil: A North Korean Christian Refugee Perspective

Juche

My research findings supported prior research arguing that *Juche* plays an important role in the life of North Koreans.[119] Specifically, my research supported Belke's argument that *Juche* plays the role of a religion in North Korea.[120] The findings showed that participants, after converting to Christianity, described repenting of their previous worship of the North Korean leaders.

Additionally, my research demonstrated an interesting dynamic between the participants and the *Juche* ideology. Instead of an outright rejection of *Juche*, my findings showed that participants inverted *Juche*. Specifically, participants hold that the government is the master responsible for the well-being of the masses, instead of what *Juche* teaches, which is that the masses are the masters of their own destiny. The findings show that participants hold the government, not the populace, as responsible for the suffering and hardship they endured in North Korea.

Implications for Practice

Having discussed the theoretical contributions of this study on theodicy and the North Korean experience, next I will discuss the results of the findings in relation to implications for practice. As previously stated, this study has highlighted the importance of theodicy among North Korean Christian refugees, as well as substantiated the experience of suffering of North Koreans. As such, this study provides practical implications for Christian ministry to North Korean refugees, both in the discussion of theodicy, and in sensitization of practitioners to the North Korean experience.

Christian Ministry and Theodicy

The first implication for practice of this current study concerns the issue of Christian ministry to North Korean refugees, particularly in the discussion of theodicy and theological answers to evil. As demonstrated in the findings and noted in the discussion, North Korean refugees have felt hurt and offense at some of the answers they have been given to explain the experience of evil and suffering in North Korea in light of the proclamation of a loving and omnipotent God. However, this research has also demonstrated that North Korean Christian refugees, similar to other individuals

---

119. See Belke, *Juche*; Cho, "Encounter"; Kang, "Lens of *Juche*."
120. Belke, *Juche*, 1–3.

Discussion

who have experienced suffering, have an interest in understanding issues of theodicy. As such, practitioners who undertake ministry to North Korean refugees should tread carefully so as not to offend or ostracize North Koreans. In particular, the idea that God is bestowing punishment on North Korea is identified as both offensive and problematic. Christian ministers should familiarize themselves with a variety of views on theodicy, and be willing to utilize whatever theory resonates with the individual, instead of dogmatically asserting one particular belief. The teleological understanding of evil may prove to be the most effective method in addressing the problem of evil with North Korean refugees.

SENSITIZATION OF PRACTITIONERS

The second implication for practice of this current study is concerning the sensitization of practitioners to work with North Korean refugees. The findings demonstrated that North Korean refugees experience a variety of traumatic events, including witnessing violence, experiencing human trafficking, and becoming victims of sexual assault. Therefore, practitioners working with North Koreans refugees should not assume that the individuals have avoided a traumatic event either in North Korea or during their escape journey. Additionally, my findings demonstrated that some traumatic events were caused by fellow North Korean refugees. As such, practitioners should not assume that North Koreans will feel safe with other North Korean refugees.

Media or stories that depict violence or sexual assault may be triggering for North Korean refugees, and should be considered with care. Practitioners should not flippantly ask to hear the escape story or life stories of North Korean refugees, as the practitioner could be, unknowingly, asking the North Korean to recount a memory of a traumatic event. Practitioners should also be knowledgeable about counseling services that could be made available to North Korean refugees if needed.

Recommendations for Further Research

This current study demonstrated that the experience of North Koreans who had experienced the famine was different than those who were born after the famine. Further research should be conducted to better understand the difference in the experience of North Koreans who fled during the famine, and those who fled and had never experienced the famine. Further research should also be conducted on the effect of public executions on children.

As this study highlighted the North Korean refugees' feelings of "othering" and discrimination in South Korea, further research should be conducted to better understand the perceptions of South Koreans regarding North Korean refugees. Additionally, further research should be conducted to understand the dynamic between the North Korean refugee avowed identity and North Korean refugee identity ascribed by South Koreans.

The teleological understanding of evil may prove a useful theological concept to help North Korean refugees understand questions of theodicy. Further research should be conducted to better understand how North Korean refugees perceive this particular theological concept.

CONCLUSION

Christian refugees from North Korea have experienced incredible traumatic events in their lives, both during their time living in North Korea, and during their escape journey. Practitioners and Christian ministries working with North Korean refugee populations in South Korea have an opportunity to walk alongside the North Koreans as they wrestle with the philosophical problem of evil. By adopting a posture of listening, rather than proselytizing a specific theodicy belief, practitioners can help create a space for North Korean Christian refugees to process their lived experiences of evil and suffering in light of their belief in a loving and omnipotent God. This research has demonstrated a desire in North Korean Christian refugees to do just that, when given a safe space and time to reflect.

Appendix A

Informed Consent Form

Participant's name:

I authorize <u>Ryan Klejment-Lavin</u> under the supervision of <u>Dr. Jamie Sanchez</u> of Cook School of Intercultural Studies, Biola University, La Mirada, California, and/or any designated research assistants to gather information from me on the topic of how North Korean Christian refugees in South Korea describe evil.

I understand that the general purposes of the research are North Korean Christian refugees describe evil based on their lived experiences, and that I will be asked to participate in an interview, and that the approximate total time of my involvement will be ninety minutes. I understand that the interview will only be audio recorded with my consent.

The potential benefits of the study are a deeper understanding of the North Korean refugee experience, including their understanding of evil, and the information gained will be beneficial for counselors, church-planters, and missionaries working in a North Korean refugee context

I am aware that I may choose not to answer any questions that I find embarrassing or offensive.

I understand that my participation is voluntary and that I may refuse to participate or discontinue my participation at any time without penalty or loss of benefits to which I am otherwise entitled.

I understand that if, after my participation, I experience any undue anxiety or stress or have questions about the research or my rights as a participant, that may have been provoked by the experience, Ryan Klejment-Lavin will

Appendix A: Informed Consent Form

be available for consultation, and will also be available to provide direction regarding medical assistance in the unlikely event that physical injury is incurred during participation in the research.

Confidentiality of research results will be maintained by the researcher. My individual results will not be released without my written consent.

_____ _____
Signature   Date

I consent to being audio recorded.

_____ _____
Signature   Date

There are two copies of this consent form included. Please sign one and return it to the researcher with your responses. The other copy you may keep for your records.

Questions and comments may be address to: Ryan Klejment-Lavin, Yongsan Gu, Seobinggo-ro 51gil 68-14, 103 Dong 101 Ho, Seoul, South Korea, 04397. Phone: +82 10 4370 7755, ryan.r.klejment-lavin@biola.edu

Appendix B

Consent Form (Korean)

연구 대상자 동의서

연구대상자 성명:

본인은 미국 Biola 대학교의 연구책임자 (Dr. Jamie Sanchez, Ph.D.) 의 산하에 있는 Ryan Klejment-Lavin 혹은 정보 수집을 담당하는 다른 연구보조원이 저에게서 '대한민국에 거주하고 있는 기독교인 북한이탈주민이 악을 어떤 방식으로 이해하는가'라는 주제에 대한 정보를 수집하는 것을 허가합니다.

본인은 본 연구의 전반적인 목적이 기독교인 북한이탈주민이 그들의 삶과 경험에 기반해 악을 어떤 방식으로 이해하는가를 규명하는 데 있다는 사실을 인지하고 있으며, 이를 위해 90분가량이 소요되는 인터뷰에 참여하게 될 것을 이해했습니다. 또한 본인은 이 인터뷰가 동의 하에서만 녹음된다는 것을 이해했습니다.

본 연구를 통해 북한이탈주민의 경험과 그들의 악에 대한 생각을 보다 심층적으로 이해할 수 있을 것이라 기대합니다. 이 정보는 향후 북한이탈주민을 위해 일하는 상담사, 목사, 선교사 같은 이들에게 도움이 될 것입니다.

본인은 대답하기 난처하거나 불쾌하다고 느끼는 질문에는 대답을 하지 않아도 된다는 것을 알고 있습니다.

본인은 연구참여가 자발적인 의사로 진행되는 것이고, 언제든지 어떠한 불이익 혹은 주어진 이익의 환수없이 연구 참여의 거부나 중단이 가능하다는 것을 이해했습니다.

Appendix B: Consent Form (Korean)

본인은 연구 참여 이후 참여 경험으로 인해 과도한 불안 혹은 스트레스를 경험하거나 연구참여자로써 연구나 본인의 권리에 대한 질문이 있다면 Ryan Klejment-Lavin 에게 상담할 수 있고, 가능성은 거의 없지만 연구참여 과정에서 신체적인 상해가 발생하는 경우 Ryan Klejment-Lavin 에게서 의료적 지원에 대한 정보를 제공받을 수 있다는 것을 이해했습니다.

연구 결과의 비밀유지는 연구자가 보장하며 본인의 개인정보는 서면 동의 없이 제공되지 않을 것입니다.

_____   _____
                                              년 월 일
서명   서명일자

본인은 인터뷰 내용을 녹음하는 것에 동의합니다.

_____   _____
                                              년 월 일
서명   서명일자

연구참여 동의서가 2부 포함되어 있습니다. 이 중 1부에 서명을 하시고 연구자에게 참여여부에 대한 응답과 함께 돌려주십시오. 다른 1부는 귀하께서 보관하실 수 있습니다.

본 연구에 대한 질문이나 의견이 있으시면 다음 연락처로 문의하시기 바랍니다:

Appendix C

Interview Questions

1. Can you tell me what you did today or this week?
2. Can you tell me the story of how you came to know Jesus?
3. Can you tell me about your journey to South Korea?
4. Can you tell me about a time when you knew that God is good?
5. Tell me a time when something really bad happened, something you thought was truly evil.
   a. How did you feel about God when that happened?
   b. How did you feel about other people when that happened?
   c. How did you feel about yourself when that happened?
6. Tell me a time when something really bad happened, something you thought was truly evil, that happened to you.
   a. How did you feel about God when that happened?
   b. How did you feel about other people when that happened?
   c. How did you feel about yourself when that happened?

Bibliography

Adams, Daniel. "Church Growth in Korea: Perspectives on the Past and Prospects for the Future." *Korea Branch of the Royal Asiatic Society* 79 (2004) 1–32.
Ahmadi, Fereshteh, et al. "Meaning-Making Coping among Cancer Patients in Sweden and South Korea: A Comparative Perspective." *Journal of Religion and Health* 56 (2017) 1794–811.
Alcorn, Randy. *If God Is Good: Faith in the Midst of Suffering and Evil.* Colorado Springs, CO: Multnomah, 2009.
Alford, C. Fred. *What Evil Means to Us.* Ithaca, NY: Cornell University Press, 1997.
Baker, Don. *Korean Spirituality.* Honolulu: University of Hawai'i Press, 2008.
Baker, Don, and Franklin Rausch. *Catholics and Anti-Catholicism in Chosŏn Korea.* Honolulu: University of Hawai'i Press, 2017.
Belke, Thomas. *Juche: A Christian Study of North Korea's State Religion.* Bartlesville, OK: Living Sacrifice, 1999.
Boyd, Gregory A. *The Crucifixion of the Warrior God: Interpreting the Old Testament's Violent Portraits of God in Light of the Cross.* Minneapolis: Fortress. 2017.
———. *God at War: The Bible and Spiritual Conflict.* Downers Grove, IL: InterVarsity, 1997.
———. *God of the Possible: A Biblical Introduction to the Open View of God.* Grand Rapids: Baker, 2000.
———. *Satan and the Problem of Evil: Constructing a Trinitarian Warfare Theodicy.* Downers Grove, IL: InterVarsity, 2001.
Bradley, David F., et al. "Relational Reasons for Nonbelief in the Existence of Gods: An Important Adjunct to Intellectual Nonbelief." *Psychology of Religion and Spirituality* 9 (2017) 319–27.
Bradley, David F., et al. "The Reasons of Atheists and Agnostics for Nonbelief in God's Existence Scale: Development and Initial Validation." *Psychology of Religion and Spirituality* 10 (2018) 263–75.
Bradshaw, Anna, and George Fitchett. "God, Why Did This Happen to Me? Three Perspectives on Theodicy." *Journal of Pastoral Care & Counseling* 57 (2003) 179–89.
Bruno, Antonetta. "A Shamanic Ritual for Sending on the Dead." In *Religions of Korea in Practice,* edited by Robert E. Buswell Jr., 325–52. Princeton: Princeton University Press, 2007.
Burns, Charlene. *Christian Understandings of Evil: The Historical Trajectory.* Minneapolis: Fortress, 2016.

Bibliography

Buswell, Robert E., ed. *Religions of Korea in Practice*. Princeton: Princeton University Press, 2007.

Butler-Kisber, Lynn. *Qualitative Inquiry: Thematic, Narrative, and Arts-Informed Perspectives*. Thousand Oaks, CA: Sage, 2010.

Central Intelligence Agency. "Korea, North." https://www.cia.gov/the-world-factbook/countries/korea-north/.

Cerci, Deniz, and Erminia Colucci. "Forgiveness in PTSD after Man-Made Traumatic Events: A Systematic Review." *Traumatology* 24 (2018) 47–54.

Charmaz, Kathy. *Constructing Grounded Theory*. Thousand Oaks, CA: Sage, 2006.

———. *Constructing Grounded Theory*. 2nd ed. Thousand Oaks, CA: Sage, 2014.

Cho, Eunsik. "The Effect of Religion on Adaptation to South Korean Society: A Study Based on Student Defectors from North Korea." *Korean Journal of Christian Studies* 63 (2009) 245–59.

———. "The Encounter between the *Juche* Idea and Christianity." *Mission Studies* 19 (2002) 82–107.

Chun, Kyung Hyo. "Representation and Self-Presentation of North Korean Defectors in South Korea: Image, Discourse, and Voices." *Asian Journal of Peacebuilding* 8 (2020) 93–112.

Chung, Byung Ho. "Between Defector and Migrant: Identities and Strategies of North Koreans in South Korea." *Korean Studies* 32 (2008) 1–27.

Chung, Byung Joon. "A Reflection on the Growth and Decline of the Korean Protestant Church." *International Review of Missions* 103 (2014) 319–33.

Creswell, John W., and Ceryl N. Poth. *Qualitative Inquiry & Research Design: Choosing among Five Approaches*. Thousand Oaks, CA: Sage, 2018.

Daugherty, Timothy K., et al. "Measuring Theodicy: Individual Differences in the Perception of Divine Intervention." *Pastoral Psychology* 58 (2009) 43–47.

Dzubinski, Leann. "Distance Interviews in Qualitative Research: Some Reflections on Technology-Assisted Qualitative Data Collection (TAQDAC)." In *Technology and Christian Faithfulness*, edited by Rick Langer and Matt Jenson, 59–76. La Mirada, CA: Biola University, 2017.

Eltagouri, Marwa. "What We've Learned about the North Korean Soldier Whose Daring Escape Was Caught on Video." *Washington Post*, November 24, 2017. https://www.washingtonpost.com/news/worldviews/wp/2017/11/24/what-weve-learned-about-the-north-korean-soldier-whose-daring-escape-was-caught-on-video/.

Eckert, Carter J., et al, eds. *Korea Old and New: A History*. Seoul: Ilchokak, 1990.

Emery, Clifton R., et al. "After the Escape: Physical Abuse of Offspring, Posttraumatic Stress Disorder, and the Legacy of Political Violence in the DPRK." *Violence against Women* 24 (2018) 999–1022.

Frankl, Viktor E. *Man's Search for Meaning*. 4th ed. Boston: Beacon, 2006.

Gebreyesus, Tsega, et al. "Violence en Route: Eritrean Women Asylum-Seekers Experiences of Sexual Violence while Migrating to Israel." *Health Care for Women International* 40 (2019) 721–43.

Glesne, Corrine. *Becoming Qualitative Researchers: An introduction*. New York: Pearson, 2016.

Grayson, James H. *Korea: A Religious History*. Rev. ed. New York: Routledge, 2002.

Hale-Smith, Amy, et al. "Measuring Beliefs about Suffering: Development of the Views of Suffering Scale." *Psychological Assessment* 24 (2012) 855–66.

Bibliography

Hall, M. Elizabeth Lewis, and Peter Hill. "Meaning-Making, Suffering, and Religion: A Worldview Conception." *Mental Health, Religion & Culture* 22 (2019) 467–79.
Hall, M. Elizabeth Lewis, et al. "Theodicy or Not? Spiritual Struggles of Evangelical Cancer Survivors." *Journal of Psychology & Theology* 47 (2019) 259–77.
Hamad, Leena. "A Language Split by the Border: What the Division of the Korean Language Means for Reunification." *Harvard International Review* 39 (2018) 22–25.
Han, Hae Ra, et al. "Depression in North Korean Refugees: A Mixed Methods Study." *Public Health* 185 (2020) 283–89.
Hogarth, Hyun Key Kim. "Pursuit of Happiness through Reciprocity: The Korean Shamanistic Ritual." *Shaman* 5 (1997) 47–67.
Holmes, Robert, and Eunice Hong. "Contextualization of the Gospel for North Korean Ideology: Engaging with North Korean Refugees." In *Practicing Hope: Missions in Global Crisis*, edited by Jerry Ireland and Michelle Raven, 169–80. Littleton, CO: Carey, 2020.
Hwang, Alexander Y., and Lydia T. Kim. "The Silk Letter of Alexander Sayông Hwang: Introduction and Abridged Translation." *Missiology* 37 (2009) 165–79.
Jun, Myung Hee, et al. "Understanding the Acceptance and Growth of Christian Faith by North Korean Defectors: A Mixed-Methods Study." *Psychology of Religion and Spirituality* 14 (2020) 445–50.
Kandemiri, Pride, and Thobeka S. Nkomo. "Factors That Contributed to Congolese Refugees and Asylum Seekers Migrating out of Congo: The Role of Forgiveness." *Journal of Human Behavior in the Social Environment* 29 (2019) 551–65.
Kang, Alan. "The Lens of *Juche*: Understanding the Reality of North Korean Policymakers." *Review of International Affairs* 3 (2003) 41–63.
Kang, Chol-Hwan, and Pierre Rigoulot. *Aquariums of Pyeongyang: Ten Years in the North Korea Gulag*. New York: Basic, 2005.
Kim, Andrew E. "Korean Religious Culture and Its Affinity to Christianity: The Rise of Protestant Christianity in South Korea." *Sociology of Religion* 61 (2000) 117–33.
Kim, Eunyoung, et al. "Pre-migration Trauma, Repatriation Experiences, and PTSD among North Korean Refugees." *Journal of Immigrant and Minority Health* 21 (2019) 466–72.
Kim, Hee Jin, and Madhu Sudhan Atteraya. "Factors Associated with North Korean Refugees' Intention to Resettle Permanently in South Korea." *Journal of Asian and African Studies* 53 (2018) 1188–201.
Kim, Hyun-Sik, et al. "Reflections on North Korea: The Psychological Foundation of the North Korean Regime and Its Governing Philosophy." *International Bulletin of Missionary Research* 32 (2008) 22–26.
Kim, In-Su. *History of Christianity in Korea*. Seoul: Qumran, 2011.
Kim, Jong Il, and Kim Il Sung. *On the Juche idea: Treatise Sent to the National Seminar on the Juche Idea Held to Mark the 70th Birthday of the Great Leader Comrade Kim Il Sung, March 31, 1982*. Pyongyang: Foreign Languages, 1982.
Kim, Jungwon. "Between Morality and Crime: Filial Daughters and Vengeful Violence in Eighteenth-Century Korea." *Acta Koreana* 21 (2018) 481–502.
Kim, Min Ah, et al. "Understanding Social Exclusion and Psychosocial Adjustment of North Korean Adolescents and Young Adult Refugees in South Korea through Photovoice." *Qualitative Social Work* 14 (2015) 820–41.
Kim, Sebastian C. H., and Kirsteen Kim. *A History of Korean Christianity*. Cambridge: Cambridge University Press, 2014.

Bibliography

Koehler, Robert. *Religion in Korea: Harmony and Coexistence*. Seoul: Seoul Selection, 2012.
Lee, Andrea Rakushin. "An Investigation into the Educational Experiences of North Korean Refugees in China in Light of Their Exposure to Human Rights Violations." *OMNES: The Journal of Multicultural Society* 8 (2017) 33–63.
Lee, Grace. "The Political Philosophy of *Juche*." *Stanford Journal of East Asian Affairs* 3 (2003) 105–12.
Lee, Yonghee. "Hell and Other Karmic Consequences: A Buddhist Vernacular Song." In *Religions of Korea in Practice*, edited by Robert E. Buswell Jr., 100–111. Princeton: Princeton University Press, 2007.
Lewis, C. S. *The Problem of Pain*. New York: Harper, 2001.
Mackie, J. L. "Evil and Omnipotence." *Mind* 64 (1955) 200–212.
Marshall, Catherine, and Gretchen B. Rossman. *Designing Qualitative Research*, 4th ed. Thousand Oaks, CA: Sage, 2006.
Matos, Lisa, et al. "The War Made Me a Better Person: Syrian Refugees' Meaning-Making Trajectories in the Aftermath of Collective Trauma." *International Journal of Environmental Research and Public Health* 18 (2021) 8481.
Mauss, Marcel. *The Gift: The Form and Reason for Exchange in Archaic Societies*. New York: Norton, 2000.
McGee, R. Jon, and Richard L. Warms, eds. *Anthropological Theory: An Introductory History*. 6th ed. Lanham, MD: Rowman & Littlefield, 2017.
Merriam, Sharan B., and Elizabeth J. Tisdell. *Qualitative Research: A Guide to Design and Implementation*. 4th ed. San Francisco: Wiley & Son, 2015.
Min, Anslem K., ed. *Korean Religions in Relation: Buddhism, Confucianism, Christianity*. Albany, NY: State University of New York Press, 2016.
Ministry of Unification. "Policy on North Korean Defectors." https://www.unikorea.go.kr/eng_unikorea/relations/statistics/defectors/.
———. "Settlement Support for North Korean Defectors." https://www.unikorea.go.kr/eng_unikorea/whatwedo/support/.
Moe, David Thang. "Sin and Evil in Christian and Buddhist Perspectives: A Quest for Theodicy." *Asia Journal of Theology* 29 (2015) 22–46.
Morgan, Peggy. "Buddhism." In *Ethical Issues in Six Religious Traditions*, edited by Peggy Morgan and Clive Lawton, 61–117. Edinburgh: Edinburgh University Press, 2007.
Muller, A. Charles. "The Great Confucian-Buddhist Debate." In *Religions of Korea in Practice*, edited by Robert E. Buswell Jr., 177–204. Princeton: Princeton University Press, 2007.
Myers, Brian Reynolds. *The Cleanest Race: How North Koreans See Themselves—and Why It Matters*. Brooklyn: Melville, 2011.
———. *North Korea's Juche Myth*. Busan: Sthele, 2015.
Plantinga, Alvin. *God, Freedom, and Evil*. Grand Rapids: Eerdmans, 1977.
Plantinga, Cornelius. *Not the Way It's Supposed to Be: A Breviary of Sin*. Grand Rapids: Eerdmans, 1995.
Perrett, Roy W. "Evil and Human Nature." *Monist* 85 (2002) 304–19.
Poorman, Emma. "North Korean Defectors in South Korea and Asylum Seekers in the United States: A Comparison." *Northwestern Journal of Human Rights* 17 (2019) 97–113.
Rausch, Franklin. "Suffering History: Comparative Christian Theodicy in Korea." *Acta Koreana* 19 (2016) 69–97.

Bibliography

Samples, Kenneth R. *A World of Difference: Putting Christian Truth-Claims to the Worldview Test*. Grand Rapids: Baker, 2007.

Starcher, Richard L. "Qualitative Research in Missiological Studies and Practice." *Dharma Deepika* 46 (2011) 54–63.

Starcher, Richard L., et al. "Rigorous Missiological Research Using Qualitative Inquiry." *Missiology* 46 (2018) 50–66.

Thweatt-Bates, Jeanine J. "Chaos and the Problem of Evil." *Stone-Campbell Journal* 6 (2003) 53–70.

Transitional Justice Working Group. *Exploring Grassroots Transitional Justice: North Korean Escapee Views on Accountability for Human Rights Abuses*. Seoul: Transnational Justice Working Group, 2019.

———. *Mapping the Fate of the Dead: Killings and Burials in North Korea*. Seoul: Transnational Justice Working Group, 2019.

Ulferts, Gregory, and Terry L. Howard. "North Korean Human Rights Abuses and Their Consequences." *North Korean Review* 13 (2017) 84–92.

UN Human Rights Council. "Report of the Special Rapporteur on the Situation of Human Rights in the Democratic People's Republic of Korea." https://www.refworld.org/reference/countryrep/unhrc/2010/en/72645.

US Department of State. "2018 Country Reports on Human Rights Practices: Democratic People's Republic of Korea." https://www.state.gov/reports/2018-country-reports-on-human-rights-practices/democratic-peoples-republic-of-korea/.

———. "Prisons in North Korea." https://www.state.gov/wp-content/uploads/2019/03/Prisons-of-North-Korea-English.pdf.

Walraven, Boudewijn. "The Creation of the World and Human Suffering." In *Religions of Korea in Practice*, edited by Robert E. Buswell Jr., 244–58. Princeton: Princeton University Press, 2007.

Williams, Timothy P., et al. "It Isn't That We're Prostitutes: Child Protection and Sexual Exploitation of Adolescent Girls within and beyond Refugee Camps in Rwanda." *Child Abuse & Neglect* 86 (2018) 158–66.

Wilt, Joshua A., et al. "God's Role in Suffering: Theodicies, Divine Struggle, and Mental Health." *Psychology of Religion and Spirituality* 8 (2016) 352–62.

Wolman, Andrew. "South Korea's Response to Human Rights Abuses in North Korea: An Analysis of Policy Options." *AsiaPacific Issues* 110 (2013) 1–8.

Wright, N. T. *Evil and the Justice of God*. Downers Grove, IL: InterVarsity, 2006.

Yeom, Hyong Suk, and Thomas P. Ward. "Integrating North Korean Refugee Youths into the South Korean Educational System: A Preliminary Needs Assessment." *International Journal of Diversity in Education* 16 (2015) 29–41.

Yoo, Eun Hee. "Learning Experiences of North Korean Defectors in Light of Cultural Frames of Reference, Social Positioning, and Identity Construction in the Context of Theological Education in South Korea." PhD diss., Trinity International University, 2012.

Subject Index

agency of human beings, 25–34, 39–40, 45, 51, 56, 142–44
agency of spiritual beings, 21–25, 40, 51, 56, 148–49

blueprint theology, 39–41, 45, 50–52, 156–59
Buddhism, 18–26, 33, 45–49, 51, 54, 56, 78

Calvinist and Arminian understandings of evil, 38–40, 52, 150, 156–59
chaos and evil, 44–45, 50, 154
China, 4, 10, 13–14, 20, 26, 35, 37, 72–82, 86–90, 96, 98–100, 105, 107, 109–110, 112–16, 120, 122, 127, 129, 136, 139, 145–47, 153, 155–56, 162, 165
Christianity in Korea, 18–20, 34–38, 41–45
Confucianism, 18–21, 23–28, 32–33, 35–36, 47–49, 56, 78

Daoism, 20–21
data collection, 60–64
data analysis, 64–66
devil/demons, 85–86, 116–17, 149
discrimination, 17, 69, 84–85, 104, 112–16, 137–39, 144, 147–49, 165, 168
divine aikido, 6, 40–41
divine determination of evil, 42, 51, 152–54

escape from North Korea, 13–15, 72–82, 85–86, 88–93, 97–98, 104–6, 110–12, 120–21, 128, 134, 136, 147, 162, 165, 167–68
ethical considerations, 69–71

goodness of God, 84, 126–37, 149–52, 157, 159–61
great law of returns, 44, 153–54

Han, 78
Hanawon, 6, 15, 77, 82, 98, 107–8
human rights, 3, 11–12, 78, 84–85, 89–96, 125, 137, 140–42
human trafficking, 16, 18, 72, 74, 83–85, 95, 104–110, 114–16, 137–94, 144, 146, 165, 167

implications for practice, 166–68
inverted *Juche*, 142–44

Juche, 1, 3, 6, 19–21, 25–26, 28–34, 57, 139, 142–44, 162–64, 166

karma, 45–49, 51
Kim Il Sung, 3, 28–29, 31–32, 81, 136, 143
Kim Jong Il, 29, 81, 143
Kim Jong Eun, 91, 93, 128, 134, 136, 154

meaning-making 54, 56–57, 160–61
missionaries, 34, 36–37, 42, 73, 79, 86, 108, 162

Subject Index

open theism, 40-41, 52, 156-57

personalized understanding of evil, 42-43, 85, 150, 154-56, 163
Post Traumatic Stress Disorder (PTSD), 4, 10-11, 55-56, 145-46, 155, 165
poverty, 3-4, 17, 73-74. 82, —4, 17, 73-74. 82, 84-85, 89, 93-94, 96-103, 137, 140, 146-47, 154
problem of evil, 2, 4, 6, 38-41, 44-45, 48, 53, 150, 156-59, 164, 167
public executions, 84-85, 89, 93-96, 108, 125, 137, 140-41, 165, 168

qualitative research, 4, 7, 11, 16-18, 50, 53-56, 58-71, 160, 162
quantitative research, 4, 10-11, 17, 51-56, 67, 145

refugees, 3-6, 10-11, 13-18, 56-57, 84-85, 104-6, 144-48

secondary evil 40-42, 45, 158-59
sexual abuse, 10, 17-18, 71, 74, 85, 104-6, 109-112, 114, 116, 137-40, 144-47, 155-56, 165, 167
shamanism, 18-25, 33, 49, 139, 148-49, 163

teleological understanding of evil, 41, 43-44, 46-47, 50, 54, 150-52, 161, 163-64, 167-68
theodicy, 4, 6, 8, 39, 41, 50-51, 53-55, 150-52, 160, 163-64, 166-68
trustworthiness in qualitative methods, 66-69

worldview, 18, 21, 25-26, 29-33, 38-39, 46, 54, 142, 144, 159-60

www.ingramcontent.com/pod-product-compliance
Lightning Source LLC
Chambersburg PA
CBHW062045220426
43662CB00010B/1659